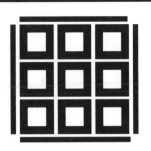

Preservation Microfilming:
Planning & Production

*Papers from the RTSD Preservation Microfilming Institute,
New Haven, Connecticut, April 21-23, 1988.*

Chicago: Association for Library Collections & Technical Services
a division of the American Library Association
1989

Composed by Karen Muller using Microsoft Word; cover design by Deborah A. Doering.

Printed on 50-pound Glatfelter, a pH-neutral stock, and bound in in 10-point Carolina cover stock by Versa Press, Inc.

The paper used in this publication meets the minimum requirements of the American National Standard for Information Sciences—Permanence of Paper for Printed Library Materials, ANSI Z39.48-1984. ∞

Library of Congress Cataloging-in-Publication Data

Preservation microfilming.

    "Papers from the RTSD Preservation Microfilming
Institute, New Haven, Connecticut, April 21–23, 1988."
    Includes bibliographical references.
    1. Micrographics--Library applications--Congresses.
2. Microfilms--Library applications--Congresses.
3. Library materials--Reproduction--Congresses.
4. Books on microfilm--Standards--Congresses.
I. Association for Library Collections & Technical
Services.
Z681.3.M53P75   1989   025.8'4   89–17849
ISBN 0–8389–7324–8

Contents

Introduction

For two-and-a-half days, April 21–23, 1988, over 110 librarians and archivists met at Yale University for a program entitled "Preservation Microfilming: Planning & Production," a regional institute sponsored by the ALA Resources and Technical Services Division, Reproduction of Library Materials Section (RLMS). The Institute was a follow-up to an earlier one, "Preservation Microfilming: Administrative Issues," held in March 1986 at the Library of Congress. Both programs were planned by the RLMS Regional Programs Planning Committee in order to meet the training needs of librarians currently or prospectively involved in preservation microfilming.

Five of the papers presented during the 1988 Institute are included in this volume. Wesley Boomgaarden, preservation officer at The Ohio State University Libraries, describes the elements in the preservation microfilming process and their interconnections to a library preservation program and other operations, such as collection development and bibliographical control. Myron Chace, head of the Special Services Section, Photoduplication Service at the Library of Congress, reviews many of the standards and specifications in the filming process and provides some insights into their development. Margaret Byrnes, head, Preservation Section, National Library of Medicine, reviews extensively some of the factors to consider in making a decision between microfilming in-house and contracting out to a service bureau. Carolyn Harris, formerly assistant director for Preservation, Columbia University Libraries (now on the faculty of the School of Library Service at Columbia University), analyzes the issues to be considered when establishing a cooperative program, using some existing programs as models.

Gay Walker, head of the Preservation Department, Yale University Library, concluded the program with visionary remarks. She looks forward to the day when a network of regional centers will ensure that the materials documenting our civilization are preserved through microfilming. More importantly, Walker sees the use of the older technology, microfilming for permanent preservation, co-existing with new digital image technologies to provide open and comprehensive access to the content of library materials to information users everywhere.

In the spring of 1989, the membership of the Resources and Technical Services Division voted to change the name of their organization to the Association for Library Collections & Technical Services, a division of the American Library Association.

A sixth paper, by Patricia McClung, associate director for Program Coordination, Research Libraries Group, Inc., discusses the process of identifying and monitoring the costs of microfilming, incorporating the results of surveys of research libraries with active filming programs. That paper has been reprinted from *Library Resources & Technical Services* in which it first appeared.

A key part of the Institute was four preparation workshops, each focusing on a different type of material: monographs, serials, newspapers, and manuscripts and archives. Each workshop leader described key steps in the preparation process: searching available records to determine the existence of other microform or hard copies; physical examination and preparation of items to be filmed, including collation, targeting, and reel programming; and film inspection and other post-filming procedures. The workshop leaders for these sessions were Sherry Byrne, preservation librarian, the University of Chicago Library (monographs); Tamara Swora, acting preservation microfilming officer, Preservation Microfilming Office, the Library of Congress (serials); Ann Swartzell, associate librarian (conservation), New York State Library (newspapers); and Vanessa Piala, head, Preservation Services, Smithsonian Institution Libraries (archives and manuscripts).

We acknowledge the contributions of the many persons who made both the institute and this publication possible. The Planning Committee for the Institute included: Wesley Boomgaarden, Sherry Byrne, Myron Chace, Lisa Fox, Vanessa Piala, Ann Swartzell, Tamara Swora, and Gay Walker. Their vision, understanding of the issues to be addressed, and sheer hard work during planning sessions at ALA conferences and at the Institute are appreciated. Special thanks are due to Gay Walker, who not only served as hostess for the event, but also edited these papers for publication, and to the staff of the Resources and Technical Services Division, Ann Menendez and Karen Muller, who tended to numerous details in support of the Institute.

Sherry Byrne
Chair, Preservation Microfilming Institute II Planning Committee

Tamara Swora
Chair, RLMS Regional Programs Committee

April 1989

Elements and Interconnections

Wes Boomgaarden

A funny thing happened to me on my way to writing this paper. I began to establish a preservation microfilming program as part of a comprehensive program within an institution that desperately needs one to save its important but crumbling collections. The process of establishing a program cannot happen overnight—it takes time.

Although it may indeed be somewhat easier to *talk* about preservation than to *perform* it, there is a well-paved road to our preservation microfilming goals, and there are consistent and well-defined elements and interconnections in the process of taking it. In fact, I have taken the liberty to quantify the number of elements and their interconnections into a finite number of distinct units.

This reminds me of a time some years ago when I lived in Minneapolis in the mid-1970s. For some reason I was stuck in traffic on Highway 12. The traffic was quite slow, it was rush hour. I remember I slowly approached a familiar rectangular green-and-white highway sign on the side of the road. At this time the Minnesota Highway Department must have been involved in a conspiracy with the Bureau of Standards or the Department of Education because there were numerous Think Metric signs on many of the state's highways. I had seen such signs dozens of times before and rarely gave them a second glance.

On this day, as I crept through traffic at five or ten miles per hour—"Think Metric," the sign implored, "10 miles equals 16.1 kilometers." But this particular sign was somehow different. At close range, it had a well-designed, home-made addendum which stated in neat, white letters on a green background: "If God had intended for us to Think Metric, Christ would have had *ten* apostles."

You do not have to think metric about this topic. I have identified an uneven five elements and seven interconnections that I think are the basic points we must stress in our rather steep learning curve. These five and seven provide a decidedly apostolic (rather than metric) number.

The five elements range from the important issues of selection, to bibliographic control, camera preparation, filming, and quality control and the necessary follow-up for completed films.

These elements are supplemented by seven essential interconnections that cannot be ignored in a good archive or library program, including the "macro" issues of institution-wide preservation planning for preventive, prospective preservation, as well as for current and retrospective efforts with our collections.

Wes Boomgaarden is the preservation officer at The Ohio State University Libraries.

And, there are the other interconnections we all face: those of cost control, copyright, cooperation with our peer institutions in the preservation process, program management, and the promises of new and emerging technologies. A concluding interconnection is essential: it is a call for all of us involved with preservation to remember *why* we are "doing" preservation in the first place. It is, of course, to provide information services to our present and future readers.

In developing this paper, I talked to Patricia McClung from the Research Libraries Group (RLG). She asked if I would be covering "the twelve steps." All I could think of was an old Alfred Hitchcock movie—until it dawned on me that she was speaking of the extensive work she and others in RLG had done in identifying the twelve points from selection through complete processing of preserved items on film. I have indeed incorporated those twelve steps (certainly not related to important wartime secrets as Mr. Hitchcock intended) as follows:

(1)   material identification

(2)   retrieval

(3)   record-keeping

(4)   searching for suitable replacements

(5)   curatorial review and decision-making

(6)   queuing to record intent

(7)   physical preparation

(8)   target preparation

(9)   filming

(10) film inspection

(11) cataloging

(12) labeling and packing

These have been outlined in Patti McClung's published article and in the recently-published preservation microfilming guide.[1]

Those of you from archive collections have a somewhat different approach to this and are fortunate to be able to skip the steps that relate to published

---

[1]Patricia A. McClung. "Costs Associated with Preservation Microfilming: Results of the Research Libraries Group Study," *Library Resources & Technical Services* 30 (Oct.–Dec. 1986): 363–74; *Preservation Microfilming: A Guide for Librarians and Archivists*, ed. Nancy E. Gwinn. (Chicago: American Library Assn., 1987).

works only. But the essence of the elements and interconnections is valid for both library and archive collections.

ELEMENTS

SELECTION OF MATERIALS FOR PRESERVATION

Put most simply, we must work routinely and closely with our subject specialists or "our knowledgeable users to identify which crumbling paper-print volumes or record storage box contents should be mummified in microfilm for the ages."[2] Just what we "mummify" is generally guided or dictated by library collection management and development policies or by archive acquisition and retention schedules, and this is based upon curricular needs, collection strengths, priorities, available resources, and, in some cases, the law itself.

Identification of Items and Their Retrieval

How do we generally go about finding materials that are appropriate for transferral to microfilm? Given the condition of our collections, it is often not difficult.

Identification might be usage-driven, books returned from loan or records brought to our attention in archive reading rooms after usage by researchers. Materials may turn up (with little or no difficulty) through a direct-to-shelf method of combing selected areas for full-scale collections improvement processes, identifying items needing minor mending, rebinding, refurbishing, replacement, full conservation treatments, preservation reformatting, and other necessary attention.

Candidates for filming may turn up on their way to the bindery with a note attached from a staff member who has implored the harried bindery preparation clerk, "Can't you bind this?—or something?" If these are "unbindable," it often means they are unusable where bound volumes are concerned.

We may turn up candidates for filming through review of important gift collections or through policies invoked at the point of acquisition, as with certain items printed on newsprint stock or memoranda files transferred to film without adding the paper piece to the collections at all.

Alternatively, important titles in need of preservation are turned up through identification procedures used in very strong collections, in the so-called "clean sweep" method, filming books targeted by dates of publication or creation (e.g., 1870-1925).

No matter which method is used in identifying items or collections for possible preservation filming, the important question that must be asked early is, what is the research value of this item in the list of priorities?

---

[2]Notes from a speech delivered by William J. Crowe, "The Prophet with a Good Memory," 1988.

Record-keeping

Record-keeping is a rather mundane but essential part of this element of selection. It ensures, of course, that your users can gain access to important titles in process, depending upon local institutional policies. But in all aspects of record-keeping, try to keep it simple and effective.

Searching

For published items identified as preservation candidates, a detailed bibliographic search for other editions and suitable replacements is a must to provide selectors and decision-makers with sufficient information to make rational decisions on the fate of the material. Selectors generally cannot make enlightened decisions without all pertinent information on a particular published title. They might want to know, for example:

How many editions were published? How important, relatively, is this one?
What number of titles by this author does the library hold?
What number of additional copies of this edition or other editions is held? What is their condition? Their research value?
What exists in print that could be purchased today? At what cost?
Who, if anyone, has microfilmed this title? Is it available for purchase in accordance with copyright regulations?
Who else holds the title, according to OCLC and RLIN, or, if you trust it, the *National Union Catalog of Pre-1956 Imprints*?

These are just some of the questions that should be asked in the selection process.

The selector's decisions are difficult, and the responsibilities quite sobering. That is why selectors, curators, and archivists must be trained and encouraged in this process by preservation professionals who can provide the necessary technical advice (saying, for example, "No, it *cannot* be fixed!") and fiscal advice ("It will cost $400 to restore this, if it *can* be done, and about $40 to film.").

Other Options

Selectors must not be led to believe by us or by anyone that preservation microfilming is the *only* option that is available for all materials that have deteriorated. The selectors must be able to choose among a range of realistic and appropriate options, all based upon library policy, which in turn is generally based upon available resources. This may include, when available:

Purchasing a replacement in-print copy, for published sources; certainly not an option for archives and manuscript materials. Unfortunately, a dwindling number of needed books are available as in-print replacements.

Purchasing a copy from an out-of-print dealer, which is most certainly *not* an acceptable option for items published in the age of poor paper (which is most of the past 125 years).

Purchasing a microform copy, if one is available, its quality is sufficient, and the format is appropriate.

Producing a photocopy on alkaline paper, with full knowledge that such copies are subject to all the vicissitudes of life in the library or archive and can become lost or stolen. With no designated master copy, one's work could be in vain.

Providing a full conservation treatment for the item, if it warrants it as an artifact or because it can be used only in the original.

Withdrawing the item with no action at all, if it is not worth having in the collection. This option of tossing the item in the dust bin may be considered a luxury to some of us, and totally inappropriate by many of the rest of us. But we must consider selection for preservation as a *second* acquisition decision—making *de*selection and withdrawal an appropriate response in some circumstances.

We can, of course, procrastinate by providing a custom-made "phase box" to keep the contents protected and together while more information or more money is sought.

These are our basic choices, augmented, of course, by the option of microfilming in adherence with preservation standards.

We Americans love choices. So we should not force-feed our selectors and archivists with only the microfilming option. We consider preservation microfilming just one way of coping with certain types of materials, not as a panacea for all things, and it is certainly not an appropriate "vacuum cleaner" for use over all other options. Clearly, use frequency and physical characteristics must be overriding factors in the selection of options for the preservation or conservation of an item.

Retention of the Original

What about the value of the item in hand as an important artifact that should be conserved in its original format, not just as emulsion on a segment of 35mm film?

In recent testimony before Congress, one advocate of increased preservation funding stated that each year the educational system of this country creates something approaching 15,000 new attorneys, 12,000 new doctors, 5,000 new architects, and 32 new art, book, and paper conservators. While this may help society increasingly to litigate, operate, and build, it does not help us at all in the conservation of artifactually significant cultural property in our library and archive collections.

Retention of originals is a very big question to answer "up front" in a preservation program. Many items can be filmed and retained without a great deal of damage. But many volumes may suffer considerable irreversible damage from the process. Consequently, policies must address this institutionally and from legal and archival standpoints. Questions of retention are difficult, especially with very limited resources to stabilize and keep items in their original format. Nevertheless, it is our responsibility to do so on that very selective basis.

I formerly headed a preservation microfilming operation in a large research library. We preserved over 2 million pages per year, more than 10,000 books, on microfilm. My good friend headed the conservation laboratory where about several *hundred* volumes and prints were given full conservation treatment in that same yearly period. But when my hard-working preservation microfilming staff wheeled truck after truck of brittle volumes into the conservation laboratory each week—to use their "low tech" power cutter in the process of cutting off spines to make filming easier, faster, cheaper, and better—they were villified by the conservation shop staff and called "thugs" who were destroying books in order to save them. And, because of the accusers' pitiful statistics in conserving those minute numbers of dainty things—we "thugs" in turn labeled our conservation studio colleagues as "pansies."

This thug-versus-pansy interaction is often at the heart of the many tough choices in archives and libraries. But even in our good-natured verbal sparring, we each recognized that both approaches were needed if we were to avoid becoming bibliographic barbarians or philistines. Artifactual and special value cannot be overlooked, and we must develop institutional policies with which to help us cope with these decisions.

As I have already said, microforms are not a preservation panacea. Microform is not a good medium for a number of types of research materials in book form because of the following concerns:

> Much of the physical nature of the book cannot be transferred to a microform;
> Color illustrations are lost, and other illustrative materials are sometimes muddy on film, but not always (this depends both upon the type of illustrations and the quality of the filming);
> Paper texture, watermarks, sewing structure, binding materials, and nearly all three-dimensional aspects of the item are not transferred.

Microfilming is, however, an excellent means of preserving *information*.

The archival profession has developed sensible guidelines to discern the truly artifactual or intrinsically valuable. The National Archives and Records Administration has issued its Staff Information Paper, number 21, to guide staff in deciding what factors indicate "intrinsic value" in items that should be retained in their original formats.[3]

Now that we have identified the very basic elements of selection to assure what can and should be preserved using microfilm technology, in what ways can we assure bibliographic access and integrity in those decisions?

---

[3]*Intrinsic Value in Archival Materials,* National Archives and Records Service Staff Information Paper, no 21. (Washington, D.C.: National Archives and Records Service, General Services Administration, 1982).

BIBLIOGRAPHIC CONTROL

Bibliographic control includes not just cataloging or providing finding aids, but communicating intent, action, and access points with the entire library and archive community. Bibliographic control is the linchpin to accessibility of information for our readers. It is no accident that the organization created with the assistance of the Council on Library Resources is called the Commission on Preservation and Access.

Intent and Timeliness—Queuing and Prospective Cataloging

It is vital that we not hide our preservation filming activity. With the increasing level of filming activity in North America, we must inform each other almost instantaneously of our intent to film deteriorated published titles. The cost of duplication of effort is far too high. This was the very reason the Research Libraries Group invented the concept of "queuing" decisions online for rapid communication of intent. It is a model that research library users of OCLC envy.

There is, however, a process under discussion that enables OCLC users to do "prospective" cataloging of intent to film. It does have several drawbacks, especially the time-lag between the entry of the "little white lie" cataloging (also labeled "the moral equivalent of CIP cataloging") and the actual availability of the film.

Needless to say, manuscript and archive collections need not be as concerned about queuing those materials as those working with published materials.

Level of Cataloging—An Institutional Decision

The purpose of preservation is, essentially, extended accessibility. Provision of adequate bibliographic controls is a necessity.

But the level of cataloging provided for titles converted to master microform must be decided at a relatively high level of the library or archive administration. Many administrators believe—correctly, in my opinion—that it makes little sense to expend $50 (or more) to select, prepare, and film a title only to give it a minimal level record in OCLC or RLIN. But level of cataloging—full, recon standard, or minimal—is an institutional decision. Grant money often, or perhaps generally, does not pay for it, with the assumption that this is an institutional responsibility that should be borne as a routine cost of running a library or archive. After all, all items we acquire for our collections must be processed before they can be made accessible to our clientele—microforms are no exception.

Preservation professionals have, and well they should, a large and increasing respect for our colleagues in cataloging. They, too, must cope with mountains of materials screaming for attention. "Deferred cataloging" is, in addition to our own "phased preservation," one of the most useful euphemisms of our profession. Smooth interaction with other technical service units is critical to the success of the preservation effort.

PREPARATION FOR THE CAMERA—AVOIDING "GARBAGE IN, GARBAGE OUT"

A third critical element in this process is the preparation of materials for the camera. In a phrase, the whole idea is to avoid the pitfalls of "garbage in, garbage out." The components of this element are many and complex and cover the importance of both filming order and completeness. Missing text should be replaced when possible. One library found in a recent pilot preservation microfilming project of published monographs that fully one-third of the titles designated by the selector for reformatting required the replacement of missing text. This is an appalling result of the heavy use, poor paper, and often inappropriate binding decisions of the past century. Needless to say, we must court the favor of our interlibrary loan (ILL) staff. Loan arrangements through ILL, or more informal personal interlibrary connections, are most definitely beneficial.

This element also covers the proper preparation of materials, including the appropriate level of identification with targets on the film, to assist readers in finding their way around the text.

FILMING—NOT JUST TAKING PICTURES

The fourth essential element is the filming itself. I am not sure how many readers have actually operated a microfilming camera, but I know it is not just a matter of taking snapshots. There is a great deal of substance to the art and science of the process.

Standards and Specifications—Their Importance

Existing standards and specifications are our friends. Standards and "specs" are there for a good purpose:

They assure us of high quality;
They obviate the need to reinvent the wheel;
They help us all avoid becoming individual pioneers;
They convince outsiders of our resolve to do it right; and
They help us avoid the errors of the past as we take advantage of industry norms and standards.

Following proper standards and good, well-tested specifications keeps us from doing stupid things, like spending $300 or more per reel to select, prepare, film, and catalog—and then to subject the camera negative to patron usage, or store negatives randomly in basements or attics where they are vulnerable to the uncontrolled environment.

Understanding and following appropriate standards and good specifications help us avoid the temptation to take short cuts. I often quote the maxim: There are two cardinal sins from which all the other spring: impatience and laziness.

What about microfiche as a preservation medium? Is it an oxymoron, a contradiction in terms, this preservation microfiche? The term has been used to describe many concepts, among them: artificial intelligence, jumbo shrimp, married life, deafening silence, mournful optimist, disaster planning, preservation xerography and preservation microfiche. Because we lack the written standards for microfiche as a preservation medium, some do consider it an oxymoron. Certainly, however, more discussion is needed on this format, because it has some striking advantages over 35mm film.

And what about printing masters—generation "b"—a second generation negative between master and use copy? This must be an up-front, conscious decision made in your institutions. It should be dependent upon expected usage of the sacrosanct generation "a" copy, the storage of that copy, and the concomitant costs that a printing master entails. With all these implications, a policy is needed. From my point of view, creating a printing master is generally an excellent idea.

When considering standards and specifications for filming, it is important to remember that much of our work is a compromise; we strive for our ideals but we cannot always reach them because of a lack of resources. But in this area, we attempt to do the best possible.

Who and Where? In-house-Versus-Contractual Arrangements

By whom and where will your preservation microfilm be created? Where can you count on operators' skills to film such varied materials as white, clean pages with high contrast and darkened low-contrast documents? As mentioned above, filming is not as simple as shooting snapshots with your Polaroid.

The decision either to film in-house or to contract out is one that must be made based on what you can do in-house and what a service agent can do for you with, of course, careful comparisons. As more libraries and archives get involved with preservation, the number of outside contractors doing this kind of work will increase.

Let me draw a parallel between library binders and contractual microfilmers. Assertive, knowledgeable, and tireless librarians have worked wonders with binders to make them more responsive. Now they are among our greatest allies in the maintenance and preservation of collections. This is happening now with filming agents, be they for-profit companies or regional not-for-profit services. They have a great deal to teach us, and we them.

QUALITY CONTROL AND FOLLOW-UP

The fifth element involves quality control—keeping your camera operators honest—and the necessary follow-up. It is essential that the film be good enough for all time because it is likely that this may be the materials last chance to be preserved.

The master negative must be stored under conditions that protect it from natural and man-made disasters. Ideally it should be used only for the production of printing masters. Many institutions are utilizing underground storage facilities for their master copies. In any case, masters and service copies should never be stored in the same building.

We must also provide access for other libraries, archives, and scholars to borrow or purchase filmed titles. For important archival collections, service copies may be requested by researchers. In libraries, nearly every copy published within certain periods is in need of replacement. Over the years, we can expect to receive many purchase requests for those titles on film.

Having covered the five basic elements, what about their interconnections?

MACRO ISSUES: INTERCONNECTIONS

SYSTEMWIDE PRESERVATION

Although this may appear obvious, preservation microfilming operations must be placed appropriately in the context of systemwide preservation programs within the archive or library.

It is difficult to overemphasize the importance of good planning for the preservation program. Such planning efforts must include key staff members involved with collections and those who set institutional and collection priorities. Planning must deal up-front with the local priorities for preservation efforts. Good planning will also address the quantitative needs of the collections, which often take the form of a condition survey: How bad, in quantitative terms, is it inside those Hollinger boxes? The issues often are ones of scope: How many linear feet (or miles) of filming candidates do we have in this collection, and how do we approach the problem?

Also, a system of proactive, preventive preservation should be in place to prevent accelerated damage and decay. It is generally cheaper to prevent than to cure. This means maintaining an appropriate physical environment: Providing cool, dark, pest-free, and relatively dry storage conditions is a preventive, prospective action that can hardly be overestimated in its importance. It also means the existence of disaster prevention and contingency plans to enable us to prevent and, if necessary, to cope with disastrous situations.

We must also fit in programs to make our users and staff aware of our preservation goals as we transfer many volumes to preservation microfilm. It should go without saying that the preservation program must have the strong support of the archive's or library's chief executive officer, because from that office emanates the fiscal support: No money means no preservation. "Preservation on a shoestring" is a phrase that no longer has a place in library and archive thinking. Quite simply, it cannot be done on a shoestring. At issue here is the survival of information of permanent value.

COST CONTROL

The second interconnection is money. The sobering fact is that it costs us real money to convert unusable or unstable paper documents to usable and stable microfilm.

But we are in some difficult economic trouble in our archives and libraries. We have many mouths to feed, so to speak, and many competing interests, all with valid claims to scarce resources. The cost of journals and other serials is escalating at 20 per cent and more per year on average. Weak exchange rates make the U.S. dollar just so much pulp abroad, where we acquire important foreign materials.

There is a legitimate demand for new expensive information technologies by our colleagues. Access to new information technologies is important to our mission and is expensive in software, equipment, and access terms.

The task of retrospective conversion of records is far from complete, assisted in a small way by preservation microfilming recataloging. It is not cheap. Also, the automation of bibliographic control systems is an important priority for many institutions, and it is perceived by some administrators as having a far higher priority than the preservation of old documents and books.

Because of the competition for resources in libraries and archives, we need to be as efficient as possible. We are faced in a real sense with the specter of buying our collections back from the devil. We must, above all, avoid duplicative or unnecessary efforts.

COPYRIGHT

As a third interconnection, we must make every effort to observe copyright laws when microfilming materials that are identified and selected in our programs. Often, the items that come to our attention are beyond the copyright protection provided by the Copyright Revision Act, which went into effect in 1978. Most of our materials in the worst condition were printed between 1860 and 1910, an era for which no copyright protection exists for published materials.

The bottom line is that all published works should be searched for commercial availability before making any single copies to be used as a replacement. According to the law, "if an item cannot be located in the standard list of trade bibliographies and catalogs ... then a copy may be reproduced to replace the deteriorated original ..."[4] Archival and manuscript filming is another game, and it follows its own rules on retention, accessibility, and duplication.

COOPERATION WITH THE PRIVATE AND PUBLIC SECTORS

No discussion of preservation microfilming is complete without mentioning cooperation with both the private sector and our kindred institutional members.

Over the past 50 years, there have been numerous preservation microfilming projects that involved more than one library, institution, or private for-profit company. Archival collections, of course, do not generally follow this route, because of the differences in their collections.

Cooperative projects are undertaken for a number of reasons, but the most important and obvious reason is to share the strengths of the current or retrospective collections. Between two large libraries, or among several institutions in a

---

[4]R. Gay Walker, "Preserving the Intellectual Content of Deteriorated Library Materials," in The Preservation Challenge: A Guide to Conserving Library Materials, ed. by Carolyn Clark Morrow (White Plains, N.Y.: Knowledge Industry, 1983), p. 106.

particular region, the extent of holdings in certain subjects can become nearly comprehensive. For example, the Library of Congress and the New York Public Library have continued to film on a regular basis most of the world's national gazettes by dividing the world in two, like a fifteenth-century pope, each doing about half and sharing copies of the films.

A short list of recent important cooperators include the Research Libraries Group with several Cooperative Preservation Microfilming Projects, the American Philological Association, the American Theological Library Association, the U.S. Newspaper Project, and the Canadian Institute for Historical Microreproduction. There is no monolithic national plan for this. But there is evolving a nationwide system that is proving very effective in preserving at-risk collections. The efforts of the Commission on Preservation and Access are eagerly anticipated.

All of this is further enhanced by tight bibliographic control and communication.

KNOW-HOW, TRAINING, NETWORKS, AND PERSONNEL IN PROGRAM MANAGEMENT

A fifth interconnection involves all the above-mentioned aspects of the subject. It is, of course, the management of the program itself. Since many aspects of the management of a program are discussed above, let it suffice to paraphrase an esteemed professional colleague who has stated that preservation management—like *all* aspects of library management—is no place for wimps or whiners. Preservation management is an essential component of sound library and archive administration.

TECHNOLOGIES OF THE NEAR, INTERMEDIATE, AND LONG-RANGE FUTURE

A sixth interconnection is that of technology: near-term, intermediate, and long-range. There are a number of good reasons why we are, even in this age of the microchip, still interested in the tried and true medium of microfilm.

Why preservation microfilming now, with electronic and optical technologies so promising, so near? Optical disk technology has a tremendous promise for all aspects of information management. But we are not there yet. We do not have all the technical standards for the recording and playback of this medium. We are not sure if we are creating—to use a well-known metaphor here—a VHS or a Beta. We do not know yet if we have what will turn out to be an 8-track for the 1980s or if this is a very long-term and stable medium.

We have a good deal to discover about adequate indexing and access structures, and about the mechanics of building and using a large library of materials on disk, about the impact of this technology on current publishing patterns and information distribution, and about costs. We really do not know about the stability of the image on the disks, although we are hopeful. And finally, we do not have the technology on a small, affordable scale yet. Some of us can hardly afford microform reader/printers, let alone new CD-ROM players.

This or any other miracle cure is welcome, as well as low-cost mass deacidification. But there are simply too many volumes and documents falling into the brittle, endangered category each year to delay. Fortunately, the selection and preparation procedures for reformatting are essentially the same, whether the storage medium is to be microfilm or optical disk.

It is quite probable that the materials that have been transferred to high quality microfilm can be easily and cheaply transferred to the more advanced technology of optical disk with little difficulty. Those institutions that have a program for routine preservation microfilming will probably be able to plug into the newer technology when that time comes.

Simply stated, micrographics is a proven, stable, cost-effective solution to a large number of our brittle or unstable paper problems. We have been filming since the 1930s. Film has exceptionally good aging characteristics. Created, processed, and stored properly, this medium is extraordinarily stable.

DO NOT FORGET THE READER

The final interconnection is really an admonition to all involved in the selection of materials for preservation reformatting and to all that produce the film: Please think of the reader or, in today's library jargon, the "end user." After all, the reader is the last person we ask. Perhaps all of us involved with preservation microfilming in archives and libraries should be required each day to read at least an hour—memos, reports, letters, books, and so on—on a microfilm or microfiche reader. This would help us to understand the reader's fatigue in reading an out-of-focus image, or to understand the frustration caused by a missing page or map, or feel the rage experienced when the reader/printer does not work. Certainly, the interconnection of our reading equipment must not be ignored.

CONCLUSION

Neither should we ignore the most basic interconnection of all, which is that between the preservation of our research collections and our mission to provide continued and uninterrupted access to those collections for all current and future readers.

Standards and Specifications

Myron Chace

Librarians and archivists who are responsible for planning, implementing, overseeing, or contracting for any aspect of the filming process have a duty to become knowledgeable about the relevant micrographics standards *before* setting up any component of a library or archives preservation microfilming program.

STANDARDS

Standards perform a number of functions. In the field of micrographics, for example, standards protect consumers in that the microform product that is acquired conforms to established norms; standards include an education function by spelling out procedures to be followed in using a microform product; and, if an institution chooses to produce preservation microfilm files, standards provide guidance in selecting the right materials and equipment to accomplish the work.

In the United States at the present time, micrographics standards are primarily issued under the auspices of the American National Standards Institute (ANSI). But they are written by many organizations including industry associations such as the Association for Information and Image Management (AIIM), U.S. government departments, and library organizations. The responsibility for developing permanence standards and testing methods for raw film stock and processed microfilm is a function of the ANSI Committee on Photographic Films, Plates, and Paper through the National Association of Photographic Manufacturers. The AIIM National Standards Committee, however, is now responsible for standards for formatting of microforms, image quality, and microform equipment. AIIM is an ANSI–approved standards organization and has issued numerous microform standards, many of which have been certified as ANSI standards.[1]

ANSI–accredited standards committees usually are made up of a mix of producers and users in order to balance economic interests with interests of the ultimate consumer. Subcommittees or working groups usually write the standards and a draft is sent to committee members for balloting. All negative votes must be resolved before a standard can be approved by ANSI. Existing standards are

---

Myron Chace is head of the Special Services Section, Photoduplication Service, Library of Congress.

[1]See the Appendix for addresses where standards may be obtained. It also includes full citations to standards noted throughout this paper.

subject to periodic review. Basically, the same procedures are followed as in writing a new standard.

Even though this overview is quite brief, one should understand that writing and approving a standard is a lengthy procedure, often requiring many years to complete. The lengthy procedure sometimes presents problems. In the field of micrographics, new processes and materials can appear at any time. The temptation is often great to utilize them without appropriate evaluation and approval. But the wise preservation microfilming manager will resist the temptation to take up the new until standards are developed that assure that concerns for preservation and permanence are satisfied.

Another definite drawback to the standards process is that standards as published in the United States generally have no legal authority. But microform standards can be included and specified in legal contracts with vendors.

A criticism often expressed about some micrographics standards is that they are unbelievably technical. In part, this is true; but the primary microform standards usually include well-written forewords and appendices directed to persons other than technicians, engineers, or scientists. Criticisms aside, standards literature describes good practice and offers clear explanations of the reasons for recommended and required procedures.

A more detailed overview of standards is included in chapter 4 of *Preservation Microfilming*.[1] For additional information on the standards process and involvement by the library community, consult *Technical Standards: An Introduction for Librarians*.[2]

SCOPE

This paper describes the rather basic points in the production of a preservation microfilm—i.e., work with 35mm first-generation, silver-gelatin, polyester base, negative roll microfilm. There are basic standards or recommended practices related to each step in the production process. Reference is made to them in an abbreviated notation when each component in the production process is discussed. For each standard referenced, there is a full citation in the Appendix. Most of the standards cited also contain cross-references to additional relevant standards.

One must be cautioned that this brief description is not a substitute for studying the noted standards. Anyone who is assigned to plan or carry out any operation in preservation microfilming must know the relevant standards. Knowledge of relevant standards is equally important if preservation microfilming work is contracted out. References to standards may be one of only a few ways by which a filming vendor can be effectively evaluated.

Within the context of this paper, the following assumptions must be made in describing the production of preservation microfilming:

---

[1]*Preservation Microfilming: A Guide for Librarians and Archivists*, ed. Nancy E. Gwinn. (Chicago: American Library Assn., 1987).
[2]Walt Crawford, *Technical Standards: An Introduction for Librarians* (White Plains, N.Y.: Knowledge Industry, 1986).

(1) Descriptions of work steps are aimed at those who have some responsibility for planning, implementing, or overseeing various aspects of preservation microfilming.

(2) There are no suggestions for preparing materials for microfilming, generating targets, or determining reduction ratios or image arrangement on film.

(3) Filming will be done on a 35mm planetary camera using silver-gelatin film.

FILMING

Filming is the initial operation in the production sequence. To begin planetary filming operations, four components must be in place: film, planetary camera, camera setup (including a dedicated lighting system), and a camera operator. The standard MS23 addresses each of these components and makes note of potential problems that an alert camera operator should spot.

In a planetary camera operation, generally slow-to-medium speed, high contrast, high resolution films (sometimes described as "sharp" films) are used. In the production model described, the film used is 35mm, silver-gelatin, polyester-base microfilm. The specifications for this film in 35mm roll form are in standard MS14, and specifications for its use for archival records are in PH1.41. If continuous or full-time filming operations are planned, some stores of film stock must be kept on hand. As MS23 points out, raw or unprocessed film should be stored (and ultimately used) according to the manufacturer's recommendations.

The next component in filming is the planetary camera, and the standard MS23 suggests a number of camera checks before beginning filming operations. A microfilm camera is a precision instrument. Its optical system is capable of high resolution. Before loading film, the camera should be inspected and, if necessary, the lens and film chamber cleaned. The lens must be secure in the camera body and nothing must obscure the optical path. Problems usually stem from dirt, fingerprints, or film shavings. Once the film unit is placed in the camera body, it must be made secure and determined to be functioning properly.

MS23 also offers some guidelines for planetary camera setup, another requirement before beginning filming operations. The area must be kept clean. The area also should be free of extraneous materials including unwieldy stacks of items to be filmed. The camera setup must be located in a place where there is limited risk of vibrations stemming from people moving or equipment operating nearby.

One element to be controlled in making a microfilm exposure is light. Proper illumination is obtained by maintaining a good light balance. Light reflections also must be prevented from interfering with lights set up for the camera equipment. Ambient light from overhead lights and multiple cameras in the same room may cause problems. Installing non-reflective dividers or shields around camera stations often eliminates problems associated with stray light sources. Light intensity must remain constant. Controlled light is often accomplished by using constant-voltage transformers.

Before beginning library material or document filming operations, the standard MS23 suggests checking for quality camera operation and optimum lighting through production of a film "test strip." A test strip is made by filming resolution charts at various exposure settings or making a series of exposures of selected documents. MS23 outlines a range of exposure settings for many of the kinds of library materials prepared for preservation microfilming.

After the test strip is processed, it is reviewed to determine that the camera system is functioning correctly. Images will reveal problems such as dirt on the camera lens and vibrations. Other checks include ascertaining that the full image area of the film is used at the proposed reduction ratio and measuring for uniform background density and the sharpness of resolution of the smallest images. If problems are noted, they must be corrected. After it has been determined that the camera system is functioning correctly, filming of collection materials can begin.

In general, these are the basic steps in a filming operation:

(1) The camera operator reads filming instructions supplied with the materials.

(2) The camera head is turned to match the requested format or desired film travel direction.

(3) By adjusting the camera height, the requested reduction ratio is obtained.

(4) At the specified reduction ratio, frame parameters are checked to see if the entire document will be captured in the frame.

(5) A light reading is taken to measure the amount of light reflected from the page.

(6) Lights are adjusted for proper exposure.

(7) All test targets (for example, resolution charts) and title targets are filmed first.

(8) The operator films materials following the instructions provided. Usually each item is filmed cover to cover, or each folder is filmed followed by the contents. Targets interfiled with the documents or pages are also filmed. Bound materials and some unwieldy documents may require the use of a book holder, book box, or cradle to make pages appear flat.

(9) After filming, original documents are returned to an appropriate location and the camera area is cleaned.

PROCESSING

Once microfilm has been exposed, it contains "latent images" of materials filmed. Processing is applying a series of chemical and physical treatments to exposed film to produce a final photographic image—i.e., to make latent images visible. In a library preservation microfilming operation, whether to process film or to have it processed by a microfilm service laboratory is one of the most critical decisions that must be made. Both MS23 and *Preservation Microfilming* outline points to consider in making this decision.[1]

The piece of equipment that accomplishes this work is a processor. It is a machine with several tanks or trays containing liquid chemicals and water. MS23 describes a variety of processors. No matter how straightforward in operation a processor is purported to be, such equipment tends to be complex, sensitive, and requires continual maintenance and competent staff to operate it. In addition, if a large-capacity operation is planned, plumbing, drainage, and ventilation may have to be upgraded to make large-scale processing equipment operational.

Beyond equipment considerations, there are other components in processing operations that are discussed in the standard MS23:

> Chemicals—Those used in the system must be compatible with the specific film and processor. Manufacturers' recommendations for correct use must be followed.

> Washing—For production of a preservation master negative, film must have an archival wash. (Archival washing tests are specified in the standards PH1.41 and PH4.8.) In addition, MS23 makes specific recommendations if local water is excessively hard or soft.

> Drying—As with chemicals and washes, drying film requires following film and equipment manufacturers' recommendations. Larger operations require drying cabinets.

What actually happens in processing operations?

(1) Equipment is made ready by properly mixing developing and fixing chemicals and putting them into the processor.

(2) Initial film processing work will require a dark room facility, where rolls of film are usually spliced together. Note that this splicing is for processing purposes only; it is not the archival splice used on the master negative to correct errors or to add relevant information or documentation. Care must be exercised to avoid stray light or handling film in such a way that causes scratches.

---

[1]*Preservation Microfilming*, pp. 108–10.

(3) The unprocessed film is fed into the processor. The film passes through a series of chemical baths that develop the latent image and fix it on the film base.

(4) After this step is completed, film leaves the developing area of the processor for washing to remove residual chemicals. Film is washed again by passing it through a series of baths.

(5) After washing, film enters a drying cabinet that removes moisture from the film and prevents the film from sticking together.

(6) The end product from the processor is a negative image roll of film—here the master or camera negative—which is usually batched in large rolls on the order of 1000 feet.

As suggested above, a key to successful filming operations is the use of a high quality film and camera. In the processing operation, high quality is achieved not only by using good equipment, but also to a large extent by keeping equipment thoroughly clean, changing chemicals at specified times, and monitoring all processor functions. Just how well filming and processing operations have been carried out will be determined in the next step: inspection.

INSPECTION

The standards and specifications set out for production of an archival or preservation microfilm master negative must be verified. Inspection is the verification procedure. The purpose of inspection, as stated in MS23, is to determine whether or not the photographic and physical requirements have been met.

Inspection usually involves two separate functions: testing or examining the film to determine its physical condition and reviewing the film for bibliographic purposes. In MS23, these two functions are discussed together in the section Inspection. For purposes of this paper, however, each function is discussed separately. Information on bibliographic reviewing is presented under the heading Editing.

In carrying out inspection checks, the operational words, like so many other elements in preservation microfilming, are care and caution. Even though the stated purpose of inspection is to certify that an archival master negative is in hand, once the negative is offloaded from the processor, it must be treated as such. White, lint-free or nylon gloves must be worn when handling the film, and nothing should make contact with film images that might result in scratching.

Testing is usually the first step in inspection. It determines if there is excessive residual thiosulfate on the film. Some thiosulfate, introduced in the fixing stage of processing, remains, but if it is too much, images on the film will lack permanence. Many microfilm laboratories perform this test (and they should) on every batch of film processed. It is important that the test be done regularly, but especially whenever any change in film, chemicals, or processing occurs.

Standards MS23 and PH4.8 describe two tests: the methylene blue test and the silver densitometric test. Both are reliable, but the methylene blue test is more precise. Drawbacks to methylene blue testing are that film must be tested within 14 days after processing and the setup is more complicated, requiring chemical reagents and chemical laboratory-type facilities.

In general, the procedure is to clip a small piece of film from the non-image leader and trailer of the large roll offloaded from the processor. Following prescribed steps, the small strips are placed in vials and immersed in a solution; reagents are added to the initial solution at precise intervals. Ultimately, a solution with a varying amount of dye will appear and is then analyzed. The amount of dye is a function of the amount of residual thiosulfate left on the film. Standards specify acceptable limits. Rewashing the film may solve the problem if too much remains. No additional work with the negative should be performed, however, until the residual chemical problem is resolved.

The next inspection steps require checking film density, resolution, and physical condition. Again, care must be exercised because this work is performed using the camera negative. The typical facilities for this work include a light table or light box with rewinds, densitometer, microscope, eye loupe, and a supply of white, lint-free gloves.

Film must be inspected for adequate contrast; this is accomplished with a densitometer. (Measurements are specified in standard PH2.16; MS23 also records the range of acceptable readings.) The densitometer is used to check both the unexposed clear background of the film and the background density of images. Acceptable background densities depend on the color of pages filmed and the characteristics of the textual, graphic, or pictorial information contained. Background density should be checked every few feet of film and must be sufficiently uniform so that when copies are made, no information will be lost and all information in original material will appear with equal fidelity on film.

When checking density at intervals throughout the length of film, it is prudent to look at the film's physical condition. MS23 offers many examples of what to look for. Obvious defects include blank film, edge fogging, mottling or blotching, scratches, streaks, and water spots.

After determining that density levels meet the specifications, how well the camera and film system have recorded fine detail must also be determined. This may also be called determining the system's resolution or resolving power. The method of measurement used is called "Quality Index." MS23 provides the step-by-step procedures to use this method: resolution charts must be filmed on each roll of film (see figure 1); the number of film generations required from the system must be known; and the Quality Index level must be specified before filming operations begin (in a preservation microfilming program the level is usually 8.0). In addition, the height of the smallest printed lowercase "e" in the original materials must be measured in millimeters. By using a microscope, the smallest possible resolving pattern that can be clearly read is noted. The number of that pattern must equal the number of the pattern at the specified quality level, which has been predetermined by plotting the various data elements on the Quality Index graph (see figure 2).

Inspection requires accurate record-keeping, and all inspection steps must be documented on quality control report forms. Examples of such forms are in MS23, appendix A.

EDITING

As noted above, the second step of inspection is a bibliographic review, or editing. (MS23 includes this function under the heading Inspection.)

Bibliographic checking requires examining the film frame by frame. Understandably, this is tedious work—perhaps too tedious to be done with an eye loupe and light box. It is more easily performed on a microfilm reader. But using a reader is at odds with the standards. Ideally, the master negative should be used for one function: generating a printing master negative. The printing master should be the film used in editing. It may not be desirable, however, to incur this additional expense, especially if it is intended to produce perhaps only one service or reader copy.

If a reading machine is used to edit or review film, extreme care must be exercised because reading equipment can easily cause scratching. The reading equipment used for reviewing a master negative must be clean and well-maintained. The rollers that touch the film must be clean of particles that would cause scratching. The optical glass plates or flats that hold the film for viewing also must be kept clean and separated when film is in motion to prevent the film from dragging across the glass.

In reviewing a microfilm file frame by frame, filmed materials, in effect, are recollated on film. A reviewer or editor determines if all targets, documents, and pages have been filmed in correct order, and if all filming instructions have been followed. A frame-by-frame review also allows a good opportunity to examine image quality: to look for faults that may not have been noticed during the light box or light table inspection—e.g., water spots, stains, minute scratches, uneven exposure. Problems in the original documents such as folded or wrinkled pages should also be noted. Reviewing manuscript pages may require comparing each frame with the original documents to note completeness and order.

As for inspection, detailed records must also be kept for editing. Editing information is important not only to document that it has been done, but also to indicate if problem portions of the original file should be refilmed. If refilming is the only solution to rectify a problem, the same steps of filming, processing, and inspection must be repeated to produce a replacement film worthy of splicing into the master negative.

As stated in *Preservation Microfilming*, the subject of splicing seems to be more fully covered in guidelines and recommended practices for an individual preservation program than in established standards.[1] The standard MS18 offers "operational constraints" in splicing.

There is general agreement, however, as to the types of splices not to use on a preservation master film: there must be no splices with tapes, cements, or glues on microfilm that is destined for long-term archival storage. For polyester

---

[1] *Preservation Microfilming,* p. 110.

film, the current view is that ultrasonic splicing is best. There seems to be no hard and fast rule as to the number of splices allowable in the preservation master roll; six is usually the most quoted number.

If film files require too many splices to make corrections, give serious thought to refilming the entire file; or add corrections to the end of a problem roll. If corrections are spliced onto the end, make certain there is an explanation at the beginning of the roll to guide users through a potentially strange sequence of materials. Note that comments on splicing pertain only to the master negative microfilm. There should be no splices in the printing master or service copies.

After all inspection and editing steps are completed, including the necessary corrections, the master negative is ready to be packaged for archival storage. The standards for packaging microfilm are noted under the topic Storage. In most preservation microfilming programs, however, prior to sending a master negative to archival storage, the microfilm roll is duplicated to produce a printing master or service copy.

DUPLICATION

As previously indicated, in the ideal preservation microfilming program, the camera negative or preservation master negative that has been painstakingly produced should be used for one purpose only: generation of a printing master negative. The printing master (sometimes called the intermediate copy) is then used to produce other film copies (usually called service or distribution copies). This work is generally referred to as "duplication."

To produce a high quality printing master, a preservation microfilming system must be planned in advance. Primarily, this is achieved by establishing a high enough Quality Index, producing a film according to standards, and verifying the quality level during inspection of the camera negative. One factor in the Quality Index method is the projected number of film generations. A Quality Index number that is low may result in a third-generation film copy (or user copy) with poor images—poorer still when those images are reproduced on paper.

Direct-image duplicating silver-gelatin print film on a polyester base should be used to generate a printing master. Direct-image print film maintains its film polarity: negative camera film images will appear negative on the print film. The polyester base is virtually tear proof—an important feature if producing multiple copies for distribution is anticipated. Use of this film is described in standard PH1.41. Employing silver-gelatin film for the printing master means greater image permanence provided that the film is of high quality and is processed, stored, and used properly.

Production of a printing master is accomplished by contact duplicating on a roll-to-roll duplicator. It operates by allowing the image side of the original film to come in contact with the coated side of the duplicating film. Light passes through a film image exposing it on the duplicating film. After exposure, the printing master is processed, tested, inspected, and stored in the same way as a camera negative—i.e., in accordance with MS23. Editing is required only if not done on the camera or preservation master negative.

In a library or archives setting, a microfilm copy is intended to be a substitute for original materials. How film copies are used and the length of time they are expected to be usable or serviceable to some degree determine the method of duplication or duplicate film type.

Although not considered part of the standard, appendix B of MS23 provides good information on intermediate and distribution copies including the kinds of film available for duplication: silver-gelatin, diazo, and vesicular. Film copies from rolls can be made using any of these film types. Possible copying methods include roll-to-roll duplication, roll-to-sheet film, and sheet or roll duplicates made from jacketed film—i.e., strips of film cut from rolls and inserted into a plastic jacket. Thus, duplication for distribution or service copies offers a range of options. In general, such copies are not intended to be permanent. They are for reader use and occasional loss or damage should be expected. Any one of the three film types—silver-gelatin, diazo, or vesicular—may be a good choice. Again, the type chosen will depend on the needs and specifications of individual programs.

Silver

Silver-gelatin print film is also available as an image reversing type; i.e., an original negative-appearing image will appear positive after processing. It makes a good service copy because silver-gelatin film is very stable. If this film is processed and housed properly, images will not deteriorate. There are some drawbacks, however: silver film is easily scratched, subject to fungus attack, and can develop microscopic blemishes; residual chemicals can cause image deterioration, and it is sensitive to water and humidity damage.

Diazo

Diazo film also can be used for duplication purposes (it is described in PH1.60). It cannot be considered as a preservation master film, but is a good choice for service purposes. One drawback to diazo films is that they maintain polarity—that is, a negative image will appear negative on the diazo copy. If a positive image for reader use is required, an intermediate positive film must be produced before generating diazo copies. Diazo film is exposed by ultraviolet light and processed through the use of ammonia and heat. Long-term exposure to light can cause image dyes to fade. Still, diazo film has been very satisfactory for service copies.

Vesicular

Vesicular films are image reversing. They, too, are exposed by ultraviolet light and processed by use of a heated drum or platen. The vesicular film image consists of small bubbles within a plastic layer that scatter light to produce a visible image (description of this film is contained in

PH1.67). Under general conditions of use, vesicular film has shown good image stability. It is also an exceptionally tough and durable film, often standing up to wear and tear better than silver film. There are still questions about its long-term use, especially for preservation purposes, and there is some possibility of bubble collapse or bubble distortion resulting from continuous elevated temperatures.

STORAGE

There is general agreement on three key ingredients that will determine the permanence of a preservation master negative. The first is the quality and composition of the film stock; the second is the quality of camera operations and film processing; the third ingredient concerns storage conditions for the preservation master negative. The standard for archival storage conditions is PH1.43; the standard for storage containers is PH1.53.

After all work has been completed on the preservation master, it must be properly packaged. The film must be wound on reels or cores of non-corroding material such as plastic. Only certain plastics are recommended and the standards list them. As specified, rolls are not to be overloaded or wound too tightly. Paper bands or strips free of chemicals harmful to film are recommended for securing the film. Some paper bands also may have strong string ties. Rubber bands of any kind should not be used.

Each reel should have its own container or enclosure. If boxes are used they should be acid-free and lignin-free as detailed in the standards. Each enclosure or container should have a label on one end showing information from the title target without crowding the label. If the microfilm is part of a set, the label also should give the item number and an indication of the contents of the particular roll.

Packaging for master microfilm negatives, although very important, represents only the first step in storage. Other considerations in archival storage include storage rooms or archival vaults, ambient conditions, vault or storage area facilities, and periodic inspection of stored film. If a library or archives has responsibility for preservation master negatives, it has a duty to store them in the best facilities. The premises must be clean and dedicated to the function of storage—no other activities, including film repair or film inspection, should be done in the negative film storage room. Note also that a master negative storage facility should house only one type of film. Other film types should not be housed in the same facility.

Facilities should be constructed and monitored to avoid possible damage from floods, leaky sprinkler systems, fire, theft, vandalism and, perhaps in these times, bombs. Fire protection measures are referenced in the standards. The measures themselves present potential dangers to a film collection. The storage standard notes this problem and concludes that the best fire protection measure is to generate a duplicate negative and store it in another facility removed from the master negative.

Gases contained in the air are potentially harmful, especially in industrial areas. Air filters can remove some air impurities. Additional protective measures may include placing film in sealed containers. Environmental controls for temperature, humidity, and air purity must be present. Specifications generally call for a temperature of no more than 70° F and 30 per cent relative humidity; actually, lower temperatures are desirable. "Cycling," or constant changes in temperature and humidity, must be avoided. Continuous 24-hour monitoring can be accomplished through the use of a hygrothermograph.

Within the vault, housing facilities may include cabinets or shelves, the materials of which should be non-combustible such as anodized aluminum or steel with baked on, non-plasticized lacquer. Wood or wood by-products are not acceptable.

Even though one may feel assured that everything necessary has been done to produce and house preservation master negatives, problems can occur with the passage of time. For this reason, some guidelines (most notably AIIM TR6) specify a periodic and systematic inspection routine. One suggested routine is to establish sampling groups in which different rolls within the sample are inspected every two years for mold or fungus, microscopic blemishes, and deterioration of film emulsion, as well as for signs of deterioration of the containers and reels. Strongly suggested also is a rereading of the resolution chart and checking film density. If problems have occurred within the storage facility, spot-checks of the film files must be made immediately.

CONCLUSION

In the initial paragraphs of this paper, it was pointed out how micrographics standards help, guide, and educate. In the context of a preservation microfilming program, standards provide the what and the how-to when planning programs or deciding to establish facilities. Standards may not be so helpful when trying to explain the why for specific actions taken. But the question why? goes right to the heart of the issue. Probably the answer should be one word: *preservation.* Librarians and archivists are often reminded that they hold positions of trust; they are entrusted with a wide variety of materials that represent a part of man's cultural and intellectual endeavors. Archives and libraries have a responsibility to preserve that record for succeeding generations. Preservation microfilming is but one component of a preservation effort. Its value as a means of preservation, however, is only assured through adherence to standards established to help guarantee a permanent record.

Appendix

STANDARDS INFORMATION AND STANDARDS MAY BE OBTAINED FROM:

AIIM   Association for Information and Image Management
Standards Board
1100 Wayne Avenue
Silver Spring, Maryland 20910

(Note: AIIM formerly was NMA—the National Micrographics Association.)

ANSI   American National Standards Institute
1430 Broadway
New York, New York 10018

STANDARDS NOTED

MS14   ANSI/AIIM MS14-1978.
Specifications for 16 and 35mm Microfilm in Roll Form.

MS18   AIIM MS18-1984.

Standard for Micrographics—Splices for Imaged Film—Dimensions and Operational Constraints

MS23   ANSI/AIIM MS23-1983
American National Practice for Operational Procedures/Inspection and Quality Control of First-Generation, Silver-Gelatin Microfilm of Documents

MS111 ANSI/AIIM MS111-1987
American National Recommended Practice for Microfilming Printed Newspapers

PH1.25 ANSI/ASC PH1.25-1984
American National Standard for Photography (Film)—Safety Photographic Film

PH1.33 ANSI/ASC PH1.33-1986
American National Standard for Photography (Film)—16mm 100 foot, 16mm 200 foot, 35mm 100 foot, and 70mm 100 foot Spools for Recording Instruments, Microfilms, and Still-Picture Cameras—Dimensions

PH1.41 ANSI/ASC PH1.41-1984
    American National Standard for Photography (Film)—Archival Records, Silver Gelatin Type, on Polyester Base
    (Note: in 1987, it was proposed that this standard be combined with PH1.28. The new standard has been approved, the number is IT9.1-1988.)

PH1.43 ANSI/ASC PH1.43-1987
    American National Standard Practice for Storage of Processed Safety Photographic Film—Storage

PH1.53   ANSI/ASC PH1.53-1984
    American National Standard for Photography (Processing) -- Processed Films, Plates and Paper—Filing Enclosures and Containers for Storage.

PH1.60   ANSI/ASC PH1.60-1985
    American National Standard for Photography (Film)—Ammonia-processed Diazo Film—Specifications for Stability

PH1.67   ANSI/ASC PH1.67-1985
    American National Standard for Photography (Film)—Processed Vesicular Film—Specifications for Stability

PH2.16 ANSI/ISO 5/1-1984; ANSI/ASC PH2.16-1984
    American National Standard for Photography Part 1: Density Measurements—Terms, Symbols and Notations

PH4.8 ANSI/ASC PH4.8-1985.
    American National Standard for Photography (Chemicals)—Residual Thiosulfate and Other Chemicals in Films, Plates, and Papers—Determination and Measurement

TR6 AIIM TR6-1985.
Guidelines for Microfilming Public Records on Silver-Halide Film.

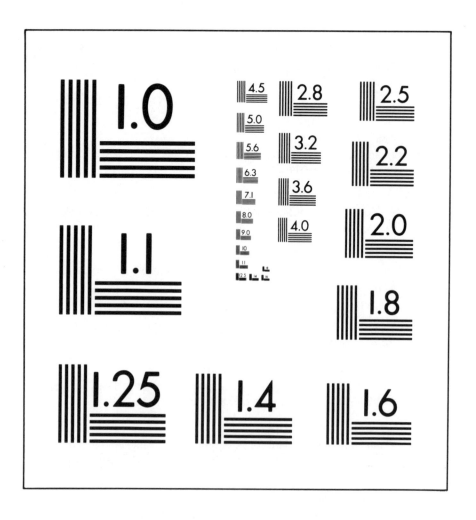

Figure 1. Camera resolution test chart
Standard for Test Chart: ANSI/ISO 3334-1979
American National Standard for Microcopying
ISO Test Chart no. 2
Description and Use in Photographic Documentary Reproduction

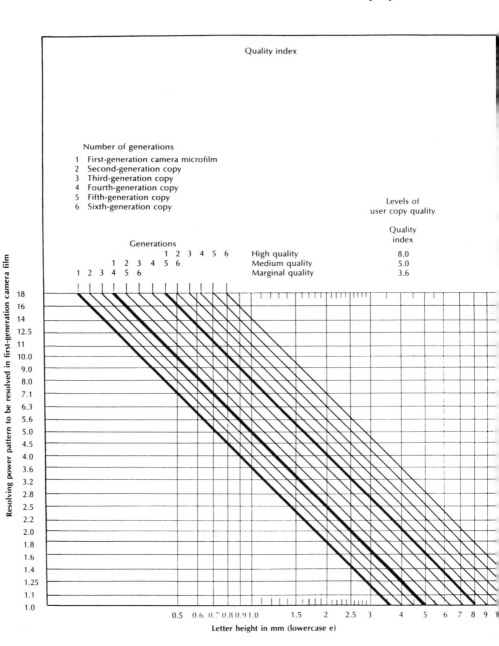

Figure 2. Quality Index graph

Issues and Criteria for Comparing In-House and Contracted Microfilming

Margaret Byrnes

I was asked to address the criteria and issues for establishing in-house microfilming programs or contracting out the work because I have had experience with both. At the University of Michigan, where I was Preservation Officer, all of the work was done in-house. At the National Library of Medicine, we are now engaged in a very large project to film 35 million brittle pages over the course of four years. Most of the work involved in that project is being done by contract. My experience with each has been very good but different.

Because I have had good experiences with both contracting and in-house work, I thought I would outline the pros and cons of each and provide a fairly tidy list of things to consider with no specific recommendation. But in outlining my presentation, it soon became clear that I do, in fact, have an opinion. So let me explore my thinking process with you; I think my final recommendation will become clear.

The list of factors to be considered is fairly long. Those I have identified include personnel, equipment, quality, productivity, flexibility, capacity, costs, management time, and administrative hassle. I am sure there are others that could be included, but these are the major categories that most need to be discussed.

PERSONNEL

In many libraries, the administration is aware of the need to establish a preservation program but cannot fund new positions to staff it. Either there is a ceiling on the number of positions or there are no new personnel funds available. This problem is often cited as the reason that a preservation microfilming program cannot be launched. If one is established, positions are borrowed (or stolen, depending on whose perspective is involved) from other units in the library. Not only does this cause resentment on the part of the managers who lose staff, but it also means that the staff assigned to the new department are not necessarily as qualified or as interested in the work as one might like. In addition, there is no guarantee that borrowed staff might not be returned to their original departments when production there begins to suffer.

Margaret Byrnes is head, Preservation Section, at the National Library of Medicine.

Sometimes a library's personnel funds may be extremely limited, but money can be found in other budget lines or through grants to fund contract activities. Contracting the microfilming part of the preservation program can eliminate some of the pressure on the institution that is created by the need to establish a new program. If grants are involved and there is no commitment from the library administration to support microfilming activities once the funds run out, contracting is often the sensible approach to take. In some cases, it is the only way that any preservation microfilming work can be accomplished.

A lot depends on local circumstances, but most of us live in areas where it is difficult to find experienced camera operators, or, if we are lucky enough to find people who have done microfilming, more often than not they have filmed business records rather than brittle library materials. It has been concluded by one vendor I know that it is sometimes better to hire people with no camera experience but who show good attention to detail and the ability to perform repetitive tasks accurately, since those who have filmed records may have developed habits that are difficult to break and inappropriate for preservation-level work. If you are retraining staff in an existing in-house lab or are trying to convince the management of a lab elsewhere within the institution of the need to upgrade filming practices, the same problems apply.

Whether starting fresh or upgrading the skills of existing staff, where will you train them? If you are starting a new lab and there is no one on staff who is experienced with this kind of filming and can train new people, the best you can do is arrange to send new staff to a preservation microfilming facility at a library with an established program. The problem here is that to develop any significant level of expertise, the training period for staff should be at least several months long. In many institutions, it would be difficult to get funding to support a staff member's expenses while away. And since many new programs are expected to start producing results very quickly (especially when filming projects are supported by grant funds), it can be difficult to spare a person for the time needed for thorough training. It might also be difficult to arrange an agreement with the training institution to provide more than a brief and necessarily superficial introduction to camera work and the duplicating, processing, testing, and inspection of preservation-level microfilm.

In addition to hiring people and providing them with adequate training, consider also the amount of time involved in most institutions to write position descriptions for new jobs, classify and post them, interview candidates, and process the hiring paperwork. If you are establishing a new program and are busy hiring people to perform some of the many other functions in a preservation department, the attraction of a contract option for microfilming can be very strong.

Contractors usually have staff with greater technical expertise in micrographics than you may be able to find. They may not be familiar with library filming procedures, but they do know about equipment, processing, and duplicating film and are usually experienced at resolving equipment problems. Some libraries are fortunate to have such people, but if not, it can be very difficult to find them. If the contractor is already experienced with preservation filming and has qualified micrographics people and good camera operators on staff, so much the better. If not, at least staffing the project is the filmer's headache, and not yours.

Other considerations include staff turnover, attendance, and personnel problems. Many institutions are not able to pay competitive salaries, and chances of relatively high turnover are fairly good. Unless people are hired who do not mind the repetitive nature of the work, attendance and attitude problems can surface. A contractor, of course, faces the same situation, but it is his responsibility to identify and implement changes in the work situation to improve morale and encourage people to stay. Some contractors offer bonuses for high productivity, for example. This would be difficult to do in a library setting since, to be fair, it would have to be established as an institution-wide practice, and funding for such a program is unlikely to be available.

Another problem involves the fact that many microfilming projects are grant-funded. The work is usually of limited duration—sometimes only one year. Not only is it difficult to find people willing to take jobs for such a short time, but also once the project is over, it is often impossible to keep them on until the next grant project begins. So you are faced with the prospect of letting go good people in whom you have invested a substantial amount of training.

It is almost inevitable that some of the staff just will not work out. Some people find that, after a few weeks on the job, the work is just too monotonous. Others may not show the attention to detail required or may be so careful that their productivity levels are not acceptable. It is usually much easier for a contractor to terminate and replace an unsatisfactory employee in such a situation. In many libraries, the process can be time-consuming and particularly painful. It can also have a very negative effect on the institution's ability to meet project deadlines.

SPACE AND EQUIPMENT CONSIDERATIONS

The costs of setting up a new microfilming facility or upgrading an old one are not insubstantial. According to the figures cited in *Preservation Microfilming*, spending ranges between $58,000 and $62,000 for a one-camera lab equipped to perform filming, processing, duplicating, and technical inspection.[1] This may not sound like a huge investment, and for many libraries it is not. But few preservation programs of can get by with just one camera, so you need to think in terms of $15,000 to $20,000 for each additional camera you will need.

Equipment maintenance is another factor. Cameras, in particular, are delicate instruments requiring repair work and routine maintenance. Maintenance agreements are not inexpensive. Furthermore, it is sometimes difficult to get prompt service, especially if you are not located in or near a metropolitan area. Even if they do have several cameras, most libraries can only afford one duplicator and one film processor. Having either out of service can affect tight project deadlines. By contrast, if the contractor you are dealing with is of any reasonable size, he is likely to have back-up equipment or contingency plans for sending the

---

[1]*Preservation Microfilming: A Guide for Librarians and Archivists*, ed. Nancy E. Gwinn (Chicago: American Library Assn., 1987), pp. 160–61.

film elsewhere to be printed or processed when his equipment fails. The filmer should be better able to handle such emergencies. Assuming yours is not his only contract, he is likely to have enough other equipment that can be used to keep your project on track.

A contractor of any size is also likely to have equipment that is designed for larger-scale production. Such equipment is capable of processing and duplicating film more quickly than that found in many library facilities. While it makes sense for a contractor to invest in this kind of equipment, it is usually beyond the means of most library budgets. In addition, a contractor will be motivated to keep up with developments in new equipment and to upgrade his facilities more often if newer equipment increases the quality of his product and the efficiency of his operation. It is often more difficult for a library to acquire funding to replace equipment that is still working but is no longer considered state of the art.

Another factor is the physical plant. A place must be found for a new in-house lab. Adequate workspace for existing operations is already a serious problem in many libraries. When a new preservation program is started, it is often difficult to find office space for the head of the department, much less room to process, repair, film, or replace deteriorated materials. A film lab cannot be put just anywhere. If the film to be produced is to be of acceptable quality, several special requirements must be met. For example, the camera workstations should be shielded from sources of ambient light and located in an area where they will be unaffected by vibrations. There must be a water source for film processing, and the water must be specially filtered and temperature-controlled. Electrical lines for the cameras should be dedicated—not used for any other equipment— and the flow of current must be constant. A darkroom will be needed for processing, and adequate ventilation must be provided. This requires specially painted wall and ceiling surfaces and specially constructed doors to prevent light from leaking. It is possible, of course, to do only the camera work in-house and contract with an outside source for processing and duplicating. Even so, it is not simply a matter of purchasing a camera and cranking away.

Given all these considerations, the question of scale cannot be ignored. As more and more libraries begin preservation microfilming projects, does it make sense to build hundreds of essentially one-horse labs throughout the country? Is it not more logical to take advantage of the efficiencies that can be accomplished by sending work to labs that are equipped to handle a high volume of work?

PRODUCTIVITY

Contractors are generally highly motivated to get the work done and get it done on time, especially if the contract is set up so that payment is made after the finished film is delivered and inspected. You are more likely to find an assembly line type of operation in a large and well-managed commercial microfilming facility than in a typical library setting primarily because, in the latter case, the profit motive does not apply. While you may have conscientious and hardworking staff, there is usually less emphasis on speed of production. This is especially true when the library is not working on special grant projects and under the deadline pressures that grants can create. Contractor staff, on the other hand, are often under the gun to meet daily production goals. They know that repeated failure to meet those goals can mean they will be out of their jobs. For this reason, the level of motivation tends to be more constant. Because the contractor's livelihood is involved, there is also a greater degree of interest in devising new ways to streamline operations, batch work more effectively, and generally increase productivity than is usually true of in-house library filming operations. This is an advantage to libraries in that it helps to keep costs down and makes it possible for contractors to absorb more work. In fact, because of their emphasis on productivity, contractors often make helpful suggestions for ways to improve workflow at the library's end of the operation.

FILM QUALITY

Whether your filming is done in-house or by a vendor, quality control is a crucial issue. Careful inspection of the film for acceptable density, resolution, and completeness of text is mandatory. Any good contract will contain detailed instructions for film inspection procedures and strict specifications that spell out acceptable resolution and density readings, the maximum number of splices allowed, and so on. Any good in-house program will have similarly strict standards by which film quality will be judged. The question is: Whose staff does how much of the work? Testing for residual chemicals, checking density and resolution, and performing frame-by-frame inspection to ensure legibility and completeness are mandatory regardless of who does the filming. In an in-house operation, once your own microfilm lab staff understand the specifications clearly, enough film has been inspected to create confidence that their bibliographic and technical inspection is being done thoroughly, and the camera operators' error rate is low, it should be possible to start spot-checking the completed film, rather than looking at every reel. The same should be true of film produced by a vendor, but the wisdom of spot-checking rather than inspecting every reel is questionable. The reason for this is that you will not be aware of what kind of turnover the contractor is experiencing among his camera operators and quality control staff. One month you could receive consistently excellent film and the next month experience all kinds of problems with poor resolution or pages missed. With an in-house program, you are, of course, more aware of personnel changes and the need to inspect film more closely when staff are new. This is one of the few areas in which contracting actually can create more work.

Also to be taken into account is the potential negative effect on quality sometimes created by a contractor's emphasis on productivity. It should be noted, however, that with a well-written contract you will have legal grounds for insisting that quality specifications be met. It is easier to reject the film and insist that it be redone at no additional cost than it is to struggle to get a careless staff member on your own payroll to improve the quality of the film he or she produces.

Another consideration related to quality is that planning to use the services of an experienced and reliable vendor can, in fact, actually strengthen a proposal for grant funds. If you state that filming will be done by X company or Y facility because they have successfully completed filming projects for A, B, or C institution, proposal reviewers who are familiar with those vendors will be reassured that the project under consideration will result in good quality film. A similar advantage applies to cooperative projects. If all, or at least some, of the project participants plan to use the same vendor, and that company or facility is known to produce good work, the funding institution may be more willing to approve the grant application than it would be if dealing with the potential unevenness in the quality of film produced by the in-house labs of each of the libraries in the proposed project. This advantage is especially applicable when a grant application is written by a library that does not have much experience with preservation microfilming. For those with no experience with it and no in-house lab in place, it would seem that having the work done outside by a reliable and experienced vendor is the only sensible thing to propose.

FLEXIBILITY

In comparing in-house and contract filming, it is difficult to decide whether an in-house program or contracting allows more flexibility. In one sense an in-house program is more flexible, especially when workflow problems exist, and the stream of work to the camera operator assigned to a particular project is interrupted. Usually you can reassign that person to filming materials for another project or to running the processor or duplicator. If a miracle occurs and you actually have a backlog of materials prepared to send for filming, you could reassign preparation staff to inspecting, labeling, or shelving the completed film. Workflow bottlenecks, while regrettable, may be easier to handle in-house than to deal with a contractor who is understandably anxious when you cannot deliver the work. This is a particular problem if you have agreed in the contract to send a minimum number of volumes or boxes of materials per month. It may be more difficult or even impossible for the contractor to reassign people who have been trained specifically to work on your project. Even if they can be reassigned, the bottlenecks at your end can cause the contractor serious staff and equipment scheduling problems and make it difficult for him to meet deadlines for his other contracts. On the other hand, it may be the case that the library has union positions that make the temporary reassignment of duties difficult or impossible. To whom the advantage of staffing flexibility belongs depends very much on the local situation.

One clear advantage that belongs to in-house operations is the greater ease with which procedures can be modified as needed. This is especially important for a new preservation department, since changes will be inevitable as the program begins to get off the ground. For example, after visiting other library's filming labs or reading another library's procedures manual, you may decide that changes are needed in the number or type of targets used. Once the project is underway, you may discover the need to borrow materials from other libraries to complete your run of a brittle serial. You may need the borrowed volumes filmed outside the normal workflow and returned on a rush basis. Such changes are not always easy to effect when you are dealing with a contractor. The contractor may be reluctant to do things that are not spelled out in the contract or may not want to modify existing operations to accommodate your changing needs if it means more work for the same price. You may be faced with amending the contract or renegotiating prices. Both can be time-consuming especially during the first year of operation when the number of changes you need to make can be significant.

In another sense, however, increased flexibility on the part of contractors is almost guaranteed by the competition among them for library microfilming contracts. If they want to increase business, it behooves vendors to use creativity and to show initiative in planning new products, designing new equipment, or expanding services. It is in their interest to increase the options available to libraries by offering, for example, bound paper copies from microfilm or microform service copies in a range of formats or film types. Building this kind of flexibility into an established library microfilming operation is often not possible because of restraints on equipment and supplies budgets.

CAPACITY

Staffing levels, space considerations, and limitations in the amount of equipment owned, can affect a library's ability to take advantage of special funding opportunities. Available grants for additional filming projects sometimes cannot be absorbed by existing in-house facilities. Tension can arise between the library administration's desire to go after whatever funds are out there and the physical limitations of the existing program. Rather than forego the chance to preserve more of the library's materials by accepting grant funds, it is wise to consider supplementing your current filming capacity with contract work.

Contract filming also allows you the freedom to accomplish more work. You are the one to decide how much you want filmed in a given period of time, and it is up to the contractor to plan for the space, equipment, and staff needed to get it done. It is unlikely, for instance, that the National Library of Medicine could ever have developed a plan to film 35 million brittle pages in-house over a four year period. It is a very ambitious undertaking and one that would have required a substantial increase in staff. It is also likely to have created a lot of management headaches at a time when the library's preservation program was just getting organized. Projects of this size are, however, possible to contract because the contractor can hire as many people and purchase or lease as much equipment and space as he needs to get the job done.

Aside from expanding a library's current capacity for ongoing work, contract filming can come in very handy when project deadlines are tight. It is often easier for a contractor to dedicate more of his cameras to a particular project for a short period of time, offer overtime to existing staff, or even add an extra shift of temporary workers when a time crunch occurs. If needed (and approved), the contractor could even subcontract the work to another equally reliable company.

COSTS

When comparing costs of in-house and contract filming, it is important to include in the calculations your institution's overhead costs and the costs of your own and other supervisory staff time. Institutional overhead and indirect costs, including the cost of space for the film lab, water, heat, light, building maintenance, equipment depreciation, and the paperwork costs to the library's business offices for ordering filming supplies and equipment and to the personnel office for processing the paperwork necessary to post and fill positions are often difficult to estimate. They are, however, real costs. In addition, the administrative costs cannot be overlooked. If this is a first experience with managing a filming project, it is easy to underestimate how much administrative time will be required—particularly during the start-up of an in-house program. Since the contractor will be sure to include these factors when he bids, it is important that they be included as library costs if an accurate comparison is to be made.

It is difficult to generalize about contract costs. Much will depend on salary levels in your area. In some cases, the library will have union positions that pay relatively well while the contractor may use temporary help who earn considerably less. On the other hand, in many universities student help is used which usually tends to keep costs down.

Other important variables in the equation are the volume of work involved and the amount of competition in the area. A vendor will often scale his prices to the number of volumes to be filmed and offer lower per unit prices if the project is large. Prices may also be kept down if a vendor knows that several other companies are interested in bidding on the contract. It is not possible to state categorically that contract filming is either cheaper or more expensive than doing the work in-house. It seems safe to suggest, however, that even taking into account the profit margin that is built into the contractor's prices the costs of contract and in-house filming can be quite comparable. This will depend, of course, on local circumstances and the type of project involved, but in many cases, it may be cheaper to contract out because of the economies of scale that a vendor of reasonable size can achieve.

MANAGEMENT TIME AND ADMINISTRATIVE HEADACHES

I have already mentioned that management time involved in running an in-house program can be substantial. I would also emphasize that the amount of management time that will be involved in the early phases of a microfilming project done on contract should not be underestimated. First is the significant effort that must go into preparing the request for proposals, evaluating the proposals and the sample films submitted by bidders, and hammering out the details of the final agreement. Sherry Byrne's article in *Microform Review* provides a clear account of the steps involved.[1] But even after the contract is

---

[1] Sherry Byrne, "Guidelines for Contracting Microfilming Services," *Microform Review* 15 (Fall 1986): 253–64.

signed, especially if this is the library's first experience with filming by contract or with a particular vendor and if that contractor has not done preservation microfilming before, taking the time to work closely with the contractor and develop good lines of communication with him are absolutely critical to the success of the project.

Regardless of the care or thoroughness with which a request for proposals may be prepared and the number of references to national standards and the Research Libraries Group or Library of Congress specifications that you include in the contract, bidders often do not realize how different this type of filming is from the work they do for non-library customers. Usually it is not until they start the project that many differences become clear. Things will crop up, especially during the first few months, that were either not understood or not spelled out in sufficient detail in the contract. In many cases, weekly meetings in the beginning phases of a project, especially with a contractor who is inexperienced with this type of work, would not be extravagant. As things begin to settle down and you are satisfied with the progress being made and the quality of the work being done, frequent meetings will be less necessary.

While true that you must invest a considerable amount of management time in the beginning, over the long haul filming by contract, compared to administering an in-house facility, will require significantly less management time on a day-to-day basis. As a busy preservation administrator, you can work hard to develop a familiarity with the specifications and standards, equipment, and technical procedures, but unless you are able to spend time in the lab, it is unlikely that you will develop the expertise needed to handle the technical questions that will develop. This can be a problem if you are newly responsible for establishing a comprehensive preservation program since your attention will be pulled in many directions. You will, for example, probably be busy drafting grant proposals, planning a preservation education program, improving book repair procedures, writing disaster plans, or revising the library's contract for commercial binding. Even without these concerns, there are a number of activities related to the microfilming program that typically are not included in the contract and will require attention. Selecting the materials to be filmed, pulling and copying the bibliographic records for them, searching for available replacements, collating volumes and preparing targets, obtaining missing issues or volumes, arranging for cataloging of the microfilm, reporting what you have filmed to a bibliographic utility, and training your staff to perform bibliographic inspection of the contractor's film will take up much time. Much of your time can also be spent monitoring progress if the filming is being done in-house but by a different department in the institution. When other deadlines loom, your project may not be given the same priority that a contractor is likely to give it. After all, the contractor is legally obligated to you, the photographic services department is not.

Another legitimate concern is security for the collections. Not only might materials be lost in transit to and from the vendor, but there is also the issue of damage that occurs during transport and filming. Adequate insurance by the vendor must be stipulated in the contract. Should a copy of a brittle book from the general collection be lost or damaged, it may not be possible to borrow a copy from another institution for filming. The same is the case for rare and valuable materials. For these, the library may wish to consider a separate contract with a vendor experienced in filming such materials. If the library already has a good in-house filming operation but wants to expand capacity, it might be better to consider having the in-house lab concentrate on valuable items and those that are especially fragile or difficult to film and have the contractor handle general collection materials of a more routine nature.

On the negative side of the equation is the comparative lack of control you may feel when dealing with a contract. The contractor has no obligation to keep you informed of his problems, whether they be equipment failures, staff turnover, or careless work which results in delays because of the number of retakes that have to be done. This is all right as long as the contractor is capable of resolving his problems relatively quickly and you do not receive an unpleasant surprise when you look at his monthly or quarterly statistics and realize that things have not been going well. It is easier to stay on top of things when you are dealing with your own staff. You are aware of the problems because you are the one who has to solve them. However, I am simply noting it is easier to stay informed, not that having to resolve the problems is a role you would want to have. As long as you have confidence in the contractor's management ability, let him deal with the daily headaches.

One concern everyone has is the possibility that the contractor, in fact, did not understand what was going to be involved, is not able to resolve his problems (for example, he cannot produce film that meets your specifications or cannot meet agreed-upon delivery schedules), and ends up defaulting on the contract agreement. This can create a terrible mess for a library that has grant deadlines to meet. While it is always a possibility, the key to avoiding such a catastrophe lies in the contract writing, negotiation, and award phases and, most importantly, in developing good communication during the early months of the project and maintaining a cooperative attitude throughout the contract period. No matter how carefully your contract has been written, there will almost always be fuzzy areas that need to be negotiated. In the long run being willing to sit down and work out problem areas with the contractor will reduce the risk of having to cancel the agreement and start the bid process from the beginning.

To end on a more positive note, consider the time and energy saved by the fact that it is the contractor who plans the details of how the project will be conducted and who has to write the initial project reports and compile the statistics you will need to submit within your organization or to a grant-funding agency. While this may seem a small point, in fact it is not. Your time and energy would otherwise be spent organizing the filming worksheets and report forms, and compiling report data. It is an enormous pleasure to be able to turn those kinds of jobs over to a capable contractor.

CONCLUSION

In deciding whether to film in-house or by contract, a library should first prepare a realistic assessment of what it wants and is able to accomplish. To do this, you must become thoroughly familiar with what really is involved. It is essential to study the literature and learn about filming specifications and standards, micrographics terminology, preparation and cataloging requirements, as well as filming procedures and equipment costs. Talking to staff at other institutions about their experiences with in-house and contract filming can be especially helpful.

A preservation microfilming program is a very labor-intensive activity. Even with a contractor doing the filming, processing, and duplicating, there is still much work to be done within the library to identify and prepare the materials and provide bibliographic control of the finished film. It may be that an accurate assessment of the situation in your library will lead to the conclusion that having as much as you can filmed by a reliable contractor will free the library to concentrate on other tasks that it is more qualified to perform.

I have tried to provide a balanced view based on my experience of the advantages and potential problems of contract microfilming. I hope I have managed to convey the idea that once you have found a conscientious and reliable contractor who is willing to learn with you, the advantages can be significant. Contract filming is certainly not without its own headaches and potential pitfalls. It is, however, one way we may be able to expand our filming levels tenfold, which the Commission on Preservation and Access hopes we will do over the next ten to twenty years. It is in our collective interest to work closely with those vendors who are involved in this type of work so that they understand our needs clearly and can provide the kind of filming we require. There is more than enough work out there for everyone. Creating cooperative and positive business relationships with microfilming vendors is a most reasonable way to proceed if we are to achieve a significant increase in our capacity to preserve the deteriorating research collections in this country.

It has often struck me lately that the present relationship between preservation librarians and microfilming vendors is similar to the relationship libraries had with library binders until just a few years ago. We can learn from the vendors and they from us, but we need to be patient with one another while that learning process takes place. We are more than capable of developing a teamwork approach to what is a large but not insurmountable problem in our libraries. I believe that the process of building that team is well underway.

Costs Associated with Preservation Microfilming: Results of the Research Libraries Group Study

Patricia A. McClung

In 1984 seven RLG institutions conducted a study of the times and costs involved in the Cooperative Preservation Microfilming Project. The study covered twelve steps, including the identification and physical preparation of materials, filming and inspection, recording on the Research Libraries Information Network, cataloging, and storage. The results, which varied significantly among the seven participants, constitute valuable data for other institutions planning preservation microfilming projects.

I n 1983 THE RESEARCH LIBRARIES GROUP (RLG) was awarded $1,300,000 in equal amounts from the National Endowment for the Humanities and the Andrew W. Mellon Foundation for a Cooperative Preservation Microfilming Project (CPMP). This project grew out of the efforts of the RLG Preservation Program Committee to address in a cooperative way the problems of deteriorating brittle materials in research libraries.

From its inception the CPMP had several goals. The first was to capture the intellectual content of a significant portion of endangered American imprints or Americana on archival quality microfilm before it had deteriorated completely. The second was to make the information about these materials widely available to the scholarly community by using recently adapted capabilities of the Research Libraries Information Network (RLIN) online database to emphasize preservation information. And third, RLG hoped to develop a management model for cooperative preservation microfilming by evaluating and documenting procedures, developing guidelines, and studying costs. *The RLG Preservation Manual* includes the guidelines and procedures developed for the project, as well as information on the RLIN system enhancements designed to facilitate bibliographic searching for microforms.[1] This paper reports on the cost study conducted during this project.

Patricia A. McClung is Associate Director for Program Coordination, Research Libraries Group, Inc. This paper is reprinted, with permission, from *Library Resources & Technical Services* 30 (Oct.-Dec. 1986): 363-74.

THE COOPERATIVE PRESERVATION
MICROFILMING PROJECT

Based on a survey of potential interest sent to all RLG members, seven institutions were selected to participate in the project, which was carried out over a three-year period. (An eighth institution, Stanford University, joined the project during its final year, after the cost study had been completed.) Early in the planning stages the RLG Preservation Committee decided to focus on American imprints and Americana published between 1876 and 1900, the rationale being that the project could have the most immediate impact by beginning with our nation's own literature. Approximately thirty thousand titles have been filmed as part of this project in the following subject areas:

Selected American poetry volumes from the Harris Collection at Brown University

Selected American literature, philology, and language from the collections at Columbia University

Selected Americana in philosophy and religion, cultural anthropology, law, and medicine from the collections of the New York Public Library

Selected American imprints on the history of the physical sciences from the collections of Stanford University

Selected imprints in American history of the Trans Mississippi West from the Bancroft Library and the general collections of the University of California–Berkeley

Selected Americana in economics, sociology, political science, and technology from the collections of the University of Michigan

Selected titles from the Hess Collection of Dime Novels at the University of Minnesota

Selected titles in American history (except Trans Mississippi West) from the collections of Yale University

The CPMP represented a unique opportunity to measure similar procedures, performed according to agreed-upon guidelines, in a wide variety of institutional settings and geographic regions. From the beginning, the project participants assumed certain responsibilities for record keeping and quality control because of the project's emphasis on designing a national model for cooperation. Besides the production of replacement copies for deteriorating items in these institutions, the project was intended to create a national resource of archival quality master negatives accessible through excellent bibliographic records and stored under optimal conditions. The hope was that any additional costs incurred in pursuit of these goals would be offset over time by the fact that other institutions would not need to duplicate these efforts and could devote their resources to preserving additional materials in the same spirit of cooperation.

In 1984 the project managers for the CPMP conducted a study of the costs involved in carrying out this project in their institutions. The study focused on twelve steps in the process from selection through preparation, filming, and cataloging to the point at which the master negatives were shipped to storage. Each of the seven institutions conducted the study twice, once in April 1984 and again that November. The institutions gathered data on the costs and the time necessary to complete each of the twelve steps for a different fifty titles each time the study was conducted. However, the hundred titles for which data were gathered differed for each step because of the difficulties of tracking the same sample through the entire process.

Labor costs were calculated based on the salaries (including benefits) for the individuals performing the tasks according to the following formula: the number of productive hours per year per full-time equivalent divided by the salary equals the hourly rate. Production hours were figured assuming that a 35-hour work week equaled 1,540 hours per year, a 37½-hour work week equaled 1,650, and a 40-hour week equaled 1,760.

Until this study, most available preservation microfilming cost information focused only on the filming step, specifically the per-frame charges for producing a preservation master negative. There was very little information available on the costs for the selection and preparation stages or the cataloging of microforms. The twelve steps analyzed in this cost study were (1) identification of titles within the scope of the project; (2) retrieval of the materials; (3) preparation of circulation records; (4) searching for extant microforms; (5) curatorial review to select titles to be microfilmed; (6) recording intent to microfilm in RLIN; (7) physical preparation of the items for filming; (8) preparation of targets; (9) filming; (10) inspection of film; (11) cataloging of microform edition; and (12) storage of master negative. Labor costs alone were calculated, except for steps 9 and 12, which also included the costs for supplies.

RESULTS OF THE STUDY

An explanation of the steps in the process and the results of the study is offered here to provide a frame of reference for comparisons to other projects and cost studies. The steps have been grouped according to the following categories: identification and physical preparation of materials, filming and inspection, queuing and cataloging, and storage. The average cost at each institution to complete all twelve steps for a title ranged from $25.81 to $71.80, with $48.20 representing the median cost. (Variations will be explained in a later section.) These figures do not include overhead or administrative costs; they also do not account for charges incurred for online time on the RLIN system, either for searching or for cataloging, which would add $0.70 for an original record and $2.13 for one that was derived from a record already in the database.

IDENTIFICATION AND PHYSICAL PREPARATION

The seven steps involved in choosing, assembling, and preparing materials for the filming process consumed approximately 16% of the resources devoted to this project. Because the project was committed to making a sizable impact on preserving strong collections of American imprints and Americana—rather than just filming the most critically deteriorated materials as they crossed the circulation desk—a method was devised to systematically identify embrittled materials in the categories targeted by each institution. Although the order varied somewhat, at each of the institutions, clerical assistants searched the library's shelflist for materials within the criteria in given call number ranges, made photocopies of cards and prepared work sheets for potential candidates, pulled the materials from the stacks, and tested them for brittleness (using the double-fold test).[2] Once titles passed these initial steps, they were charged at the circulation office to the preservation unit. These procedures comprise steps 1 through 3 in the cost study, that is, title identification, retrieval, and preparation of circulation records. Because these steps could be performed by less expensive clerical or student staff in a short period of time, the median cost per title was less than $1 for all three steps.

The searching part of the project was more complex. While all participating institutions agreed to search the same basic tools (*The National Register of Microform Masters*, University Microfilm's *Books on Demand*, *Guide to Microforms in Print*, *The New York Public Library Register of Microform Masters*, and the RLIN system) some institutions elected to search additional sources because of their particular subject areas. In addition, the "hit rates"—that is, the incidence of finding a reprint or another film—varied dramatically depending on the subject area. Sixty percent of the American literature titles searched at Columbia had been filmed already, while less than 1% of Minnesota's dime novels and 8% of Brown's poetry collection had been filmed previously. The hit rate for American history materials was approximately 25% at both Yale and Berkeley. Michigan's average hit rate for its social science and technology materials was also 25%. The subject areas searched at the New York Public Library, including law, philosophy, religion, medicine, and cultural anthropology, ranged between 9% and 15%, with an average of 12%. The hit rate, as well as the number of sources checked, had a significant impact on the searching costs incurred.

In most institutions the curatorial review step occurred after the searching was completed. Curators or bibliographers reviewed the materials to determine whether they were appropriate to film or to retain in hard copy after filming. The criteria varied depending on the collections. For example, while it was deemed important to preserve all variant editions of American fiction, that was rarely necessary for social science or history books. The Harris poetry collection at Brown University, the Hess dime novel collection at the University of Minnesota, and the Bancroft history materials at the University of California–Berkeley required little curatorial time because the decision was made at the outset to film the entire collection (falling within the appropriate imprint dates) unless condition or format dictated otherwise. The median cost per title for curatorial review in all participating institutions amounted to $0.41.

The physical preparation part of the process, as well as the preparation of targets to be filmed with the items, included a number of important—and often time-consuming—operations. Although the condition of the materials and local policies contributed to variations in the routines from one institution to another, in general the libraries measured the following activities for the cost study:

- page by page collation and flagging of volumes with any special instructions
- minor repairs; ordering of missing or damaged pages when necessary
- computation of length of reel based on number of pages or volumes
- brittleness testing (unless it was done at the retrieval step 2)
- disbinding of volumes, removal of bindings (optional)
- preparation of bibliographic and eye-legible targets as needed; insertion in appropriate places in the volume
- insertion of standard targets or markers to indicate where the filmer should put them, e.g., "Start," "End of title", "End of reel"
- insertion of copy catalog cards for filming
- delivery of materials to filmer
- completion of paperwork to prepare materials for cataloging; sorting of forms and filing of cards after cataloging

At an institution where the materials did not require several of these steps (the books were in relatively good condition, they were not being disbound, and the filmer calculated the reel breaks), identification and physical preparation took approximately 7 minutes per title of a student employee's time. At an institution where the materials required extensive preparation, these steps took slightly more than 50 minutes per title of a paraprofessional's time. The median time for these procedures was 36.6 minutes, and the median cost amounted to $5.28.

Filming and Inspection

The project managers developed film specifications and guidelines for quality control based on the National Information Standards Organization (NISO) standards and Library of Congress practice to ensure the production of archival quality microfilm and compatible procedures.[3] In addition, they all used the same forms for project work sheets and quality control sheets to assist in the compilation of comparable management data. Five institutions performed their filming within the library, and two used commercial service bureaus. Most libraries contracted with commercial operations for at least one of the processing and duplication services as well as the chemical testing. The filming figures include the following procedures:

- camera work to film the title and appropriate targets

- processing and printing of three generations of film (including a master negative, a printing master, and a positive service copy)
- set up, clean up, record keeping, and technical inspection (density readings and averaging, microscope examinations for resolution, frame-by-frame inspection)
- completion of corrections and splicing, if necessary
- box labeling; reel wind up; routine equipment adjustments; returning books, targets, and film to preservation office.

The filming costs ranged from a low of $0.18 per frame to a high of $0.34 for the production of three generations of film. In most cases it was possible to film two pages per frame.

In addition to the technical inspection performed by the filming agent, the preservation unit conducted another inspection for both technical and bibliographic quality. If the initial inspections of 100% of the film revealed no problems, then inspections were performed on (at least) a 10% sample from each shipment. This inspection averaged one to seven minutes per title, with a median cost of $1.44.

QUEUING AND CATALOGING

To understand the costs related to cataloging, some background on the Research Libraries Information Network (RLIN) system and RLG policies is necessary. Because the RLG Preservation Program places a strong emphasis on the accessibility of preservation information online, with Andrew W. Mellon funds made available to the New York Public Library, the RLIN system was enhanced in 1981 to highlight information about microforms contained in the 007 field on the MARC record. A special feature called the queuing date (QD) field, enabling libraries to indicate their intention to film a particular title as soon as that decision is made, was also added to the system. These features make it very easy to search for either queued or filmed materials recorded on RLIN and also serve to conserve resources by minimizing unnecessary duplicate preservation filming.

Furthermore, in an attempt to reduce cataloging costs and increase the number of retrospective bibliographic records in the RLIN system, RLG adopted a cataloging standard for retrospective conversion of catalog records, which libraries may use rather than full AACR2 cataloging. Essentially, this *recon standard*, as it is called, allows cataloging to be based on existing catalog card records and does not require the cataloger to work from the book (or any other format) itself.

The figures in the cost study reflect the fact that at the time the decision to film was made, all participating institutions were required to enter a brief record in RLIN along with a date in the queuing date field to notify other libraries. The use of the recon standard for cataloging was optional; however, it was used by five of the seven participants. Cataloging and queuing times combined ranged as low as 23 minutes and as high as 66 minutes per title. The median cost for these activities was $5.60.

STORAGE

To ensure that the 30,000 master negatives produced as part of this project are stored under optimal conditions, they are kept in a private vault, which RLG leases from the National Underground Storage (NUS) in Boyers, Pennsylvania. Located in a renovated limestone mine, the vault has been specially equipped and is continually monitored to maintain the temperature at 60°F and the relative humidity at 35%. Prices for this type of storage vary depending on the number of reels to be stored, the exact specifications, and the company. In 1986 the annual rental fee per drawer in the common storage space at NUS (with a minimum of 20 drawers, each of which holds 40 to 42 reels) was approximately $30. The smallest vault (600 cubic feet) rents for $3,300 per year plus the one-time purchase price for drawers of approximately $25 apiece. The RLG vault is 863 cubic feet and rents for $4,746 per year. It has capacity for approximately 17,440 rolls of 35mm microfilm.

The cost study does not account for these storage costs since they are ongoing fees treated as overhead expenses. However, the costs for labels, mailing cartons, and shipping to the facility were calculated as were those for the related labor expenses. The median time spent on this activity was 1.75 minutes per title (with an average of 3 titles per reel), and the median cost per title for labor and supplies was $0.15.

VARIATIONS IN COSTS AMONG THE SEVEN PARTICIPANTS

The costs and times involved for each of these twelve steps at the participating institutions varied widely. Table 1 summarizes the ranges in time spent for each step and also gives the median time for that activity across all project participants; table 2 reports on the average high, low,

TABLE 1

AVERAGE TIME SPENT ON STEPS IN THE RLG
COOPERATIVE PRESERVATION MICROFILMING PROJECT

For 100 Titles	low	Time (in minutes) high	median
1. Title identification	.4	5.2	1.4
2. Retrieval	.5	4	1.8
3. Circulation records	.9	5.4	1.9
4. Searching	1	19.4	5.5
5. Curatorial review	.3	3.2	1.1
6. Queuing	4.3	16.5	14.4
7. Physical preparation	4.9	44.5	21.6
8. Target preparation	2.3	26.9	8.3
9. Filming	50	186.5	117.1
10. Film inspection	1.2	13.9	6.7
11. Cataloging	8.3	60	17.3
12. Labeling/packing	.3	7.7	1.8

TABLE 2

AVERAGE COSTS FOR STEPS IN THE RLG
COOPERATIVE PRESERVATION MICROFILMING PROJECT

Institutional per Title Averages:	Costs (in dollars and cents)		
	low	high	median
1. Title identification	.09	1.09	.29
2. Retrieval	.03	.76	.19
3. Circulation records	.07	.78	.32
4. Searching	.06	1.69	.65
5. Curatorial review	.07	1.12	.41
6. Queuing	.45	3.32	2.59
7. Physical preparation	.50	7.74	3.76
8. Target preparation	.23	3.85	1.52
9. Filming	16.75	47.14	31.91
Filming costs figured on a per frame basis:	.18	.34	.26
10. Film inspection	.19	2.94	1.44
11. Cataloging	1.96	19.70	3.01
12. Labeling/packing	.11	1.68	.15

and median costs. A number of factors contributed to the variations, including the nature of the materials themselves, labor costs in a given geographical area, and institutional practices for such activities as the level of cataloging, local requirements for card catalog representation, and whether filming was done in-house or by a commercial service bureau.

The category of materials to be filmed represented the most significant variable among the seven projects. Because filming costs accounted for between 45% and 78% of the total costs, the number of frames per title made a dramatic difference in the costs. Certain collections such as the Harris collection at Brown and the Hess collection at the University of Minnesota consisted of books with far fewer pages per title than, for example, the social science monographs at Michigan or the American history materials at Yale. The average number of frames per title at participating institutions ranged from 49.5 to 197.6.

Other variables inherent in the nature of the materials were their conditions (which influenced the amount of preparation and filming time required), their subject area (which affected the amount of searching time necessary to verify that films were not available), and the relative ease with which they could be identified, retrieved, and approved for filming. It is usually much less expensive to film a special collection of monographs already preselected and housed in one location than to work through a shelflist or other screening process, retrieve materials from all over a library (or campus), and subject them to item-by-item review by curatorial staff.

The available labor and the cost of that labor also contributed to the cost differential from one institution to another. For example, student labor at the University of Michigan was readily available and relatively inexpensive compared to unionized full-time employees at the New York Public Library. Throughout ten of the twelve steps in the preservation microfilming process, labor makes up virtually 100% of the costs calculated in this study. (The steps with a significant supplies component included filming and packing/shipping.) Consequently, the market rate salaries in a given area or institution for positions such as curators, project managers, catalogers, camera operators, and clerical assistants had a significant impact on the average costs, as did the speed with which each of them was able to complete required tasks.

Finally, institutional practices also contributed to the cost differential. At the two institutions which elected to do full AACR2 cataloging of the preservation microfilm, it took approximately one hour per title (using a combination of paraprofessional and professional time) and constituted almost 30% of the total dollars spent at those institutions on the project. In contrast, at the other five locations all of which used paraprofessional or student staff to catalog at the RLG recon level, the percent of the total costs attributable to cataloging was in the 8% to 15% range and took a median time of 29 minutes per title. (These cataloging calculations include the queuing step of the process as well as the final cataloging of the completed film.)

As to the variation in costs between filming done within an institution and filming done by a commercial service bureau, this particular study does not demonstrate a wide cost differential. The two institutions which used commercial service bureaus (one for profit, one not-for-profit) paid $0.33 and $0.34 per frame, respectively, for all filming expenses to produce three generations of microfilm (a master negative, printing master, and service copy). The institutions with in-house facilities calculated per frame costs between $0.18 and $0.28 per frame. It is significant, however, that none of these figures are perfectly analogous to the others. There are discrepancies in the degree to which institutions factored overhead costs into these numbers and whether or not the individual photoservices unit reported a flat rate charged for all filming or was able to calculate exactly what was expended on the particular project. Other factors influencing the filming costs included volume (the number of titles processed at each institution for the project), the ability to streamline procedures, the condition of the materials, whether the bindings had been removed for filming (adding to the preparation time but speeding up the filming time), and the skill of the staff.

Although not a significant factor in the overall costs, the amount of time and money expended on the preparation of targets for filming with the items nevertheless represents one of the most dramatic illustrations of the way in which local practices can affect the costs. At least one institution prepared bibliographic targets using student labor to hand letter them. This procedure cost $0.23 per title. The majority of the institutions preferred printed targets (prepared by several different methods) and included more targets to assist the reader in using the film and to account for anything unusual about the film (such as missing or mutilated pages or illustrations filmed at the end). Consequently the costs among the seven institutions ranged from an average of $1 to almost $4 per title.

However, there is more at issue here than costs, and the implications extend beyond target preparation to all aspects of the process. The real question is, how does one strike a balance between the quality of the final product and the costs associated with adhering to high standards and facilitating the patron's use of the film? While this study could not produce clear-cut answers to this somewhat rhetorical question, it, at least, provided more information for managers to use in making decisions about specific local procedures.

BENEFITS OF THE STUDY

This project provided a unique opportunity to survey costs for producing archival quality microfilm at seven different institutions using mutually agreed-upon procedures and standards. By offering more information on the subject of costs, the study enabled the project managers to consider possibilities for reducing costs based on their individual experiences and that of their colleagues.

These insights led to a revision of the project guidelines (as reflected in the second edition of the *RLG Preservation Manual*) as well as to adjustments in some local procedures. Once it was established that any of the bibliographic sources consulted during the search process yielded a hit rate of 10% or less, checking was discontinued. Savings realized from less searching should more than offset the occasional duplicate film which results from the relaxed standard. The installation of RLIN terminals in several of the preservation units involved in the project made it more convenient, and therefore cheaper to search, queue, and catalog the materials.

To streamline the preparation step the requirement for page-by-page collation was eliminated for most volumes that appeared, after a quick inspection, to be intact. In addition, the practice of erasing stray marks on pages and mending tears was discontinued except when the legibility of the text was severely affected. And multiple targets indicating specific collation problems throughout a volume were replaced by one target at the beginning to indicate ''Best Copy Available'' or ''Filmed as Bound.'' In the future several institutions plan to produce targets using microcomputers, which should reduce the costs even further.

The results of the study do not constitute a basis for direct correlations in estimating costs for other projects. They can, however, provide a general framework for cost predictions. For example, in similar projects, one could assume that the filming costs (which can be easily calculated by using a filmer's per frame estimate in combination with a projection as to the total number of pages to be filmed) constitute between 45% and 78% of the total costs.

Estimates for the other steps in the process can usually be derived by analyzing the collections to be filmed. How much searching will be needed to determine whether an item has been filmed? To what extent will curatorial review be necessary? What level of cataloging is required? What are the staffing needs and requisite salaries? In most instances, it is worthwhile to conduct time studies of a small sample of the materials for steps with potentially significant variables, such as searching, preparation, and cataloging. Local labor costs can then be calculated according to the time figures. The appendix includes a formula along these lines that has proved useful in making estimates for other RLG preservation projects.

CONCLUSION

This study represents one systematic attempt to document the costs associated with all steps involved in the production of archival quality preservation microfilm. Aspects of this project, as well as local complexities at each participating institution, may not apply in other projects. More than anything else, the diversity of results and special circumstances that existed among the seven institutions participating in the same project argue against the existence of a typical project on which others can base their own estimates. Nevertheless, as other studies are undertaken and made available, they can, in combination with this one, begin to establish a reservoir of data so that more informed costs estimates will be possible.

REFERENCES AND NOTES

1. Research Libraries Group, *RLG Preservation Manual.* 2d ed. (Stanford, Calif.: Research Libraries Group, 1986). References in this article are to the second edition, although the first edition was used in the project.
2. For an explanation of the test for embrittlement see Gay Walker and others, ''The Yale Survey: A Large-Scale Study of Book Deterioration in the Yale University Library,'' *College & Research Libraries* 46:119 (Mar. 1985).
3. See Library of Congress, Preservation Microfilming Office, *Processing Manual* rev. 1981 by Tamara Swora and Bohdan Yasinsky. (Washington, D.C.: Library of Congress, 1981). The ANSI (later NISO) standards consulted in the preparation of the guidelines and specifications are cited in *RLG Preservation Manual* (see ref. 1), p.21.

APPENDIX A
WORK SHEET FOR ESTIMATING PROJECT COSTS

It often is necessary to prepare a projected budget, either for a grant proposal or for internal budget planning, before embarking on a preservation microfilming project. This work sheet provides a framework that can be adapted depending upon the particular circumstances. It is meant to be suggestive rather than prescriptive. Many of the steps apply only to typical book format library materials and will not apply to archival or manuscript materials.

A. Define and figure the size of the entire target population *before* the searching and curatorial review steps occur (this step will probably require a sample study).
   1—Total number of volumes in the proposed collection   = _____ (1)
   2—Total number of titles in the proposed collection   = _____ (2)

B. Estimate the percentage of materials expected to be eliminated by curatorial review (this step may require a sample study).
   3—Estimated percentage expected to be eliminated by review process   = _____ (3)

C. Anticipate the searching hit rate, that is, the percentage of titles expected to be available on film, fiche, or other format. It probably will be necessary to conduct a pilot search project to document this percentage. In the RLG project alone the hit rate ranged as low as 1% and as high as 60%, depending on the target and search strategy.
   4—Estimated searching hit rate percentage   = _____ (4)
   (Depending on the project, it may be advisable to switch the order of steps 3 and 4. Some curators will prefer to review materials after they have been searched while others will be able to screen materials before the searching step.)

D. Reduce the numbers in steps 1 and 2 first by the percentage in 3, then by the percentage in 4.
   5—Number of volumes to be filmed   = _____ (5)
   6—Number of titles to be filmed   = _____ (6)
   6a—Calculate average number of volumes per title   = _____ (6a)
   <Divide number of volumes by number of titles.>

E. Estimate the local costs per title for prefilming activities (identification, searching, preparation, and curatorial review). Estimate times for each step and then costs, based on the level of staff performing each step.
   7—Estimated prefilming costs per title   = _____ (7)
   7a—Prefilming cost per title converted to per volume   = _____ (7a)*

F. Estimate the amount of time it will take to catalog each title. Consider whether the item already has been cataloged, whether the record is already online (where applicable), whether the original needs to be withdrawn from the collection, the standard of cataloging to be applied, level of staff to be assigned to the task, etc.
   <The average time for this step ranged from 23 to 66 minutes in the RLG project, which also included queuing the title on the RLIN system at the time the decision was made, and then later updating that record.>
   8—Cataloging cost per title   = _____ (8)
   8a—Cataloging cost per volume   = _____ (8a)*

G. Calculate the average number of pages per volume among those in the to-be-filmed category (a sample study is usually necessary)
   9—Average number pages per volume   = _____ (9)

H. Get an estimate from the filmer, whether internal or external, for the per frame cost of producing master negative and service copy (and duplicate negative, if applicable). This should include all charges from filmer, e.g., inspection, supplies, labor, etc.
   10—Per frame filming charge   = _____ (10)

I. Unless filming newspapers or other oversized materials, allow two pages per frame. When calculating per volume costs for filming and producing all required generations.
   11—<9> ÷ 2 × <10> = per volume filming costs   = _____ (11)*

J. Calculate local inspection costs (filmer's inspection costs should be included under H). <Based on RLG project, local inspection may take between 5 and 15 minutes per title depending on number of frames.>
   12—Local inspection costs per volume   = _____ (12)*

Add * items to arrive at an approximate cost per volume.

Cooperative Approaches to Preservation Microfilming

Carolyn Harris

Robert Hayes, dean of the UCLA School of Library Science, in his recent paper written for the Council on Library Resources, estimates that there are 3.3 million volumes in academic research libraries that are brittle and should be microfilmed for preservation purposes.[1] At $60 per volume that would cost $198 million. However, I think that total is very small and does not take into account all the materials outside of research libraries. There are millions of volumes in historical and archival depositories, such as county record offices, which contain equally important and valuable resources.

When you consider those numbers, it becomes obvious that no one institution (except, perhaps, the federal government) can solve the problem once and for all, and that only through concerted effort, i.e., cooperation and collaboration, can a large number of embrittled materials be preserved. The best way to cooperate, or whether we need to cooperate at all, is not so obvious. We know how to run a project, what the standards are, and how to use our bibliographic networks (RLIN—with both its records and the conspectus for identifying important collections and for the preservation scope notes—and OCLC) to avoid duplication. Having the *National Register of Microform Masters* online will also help solve the problem of duplication on a title-by-title basis.

We must work toward a rational division of labor on a national level. In the absence of a centralized plan, we need to work cooperatively on a decentralized basis.

There is a definition of cooperation that illustrates why I think we should work together. The definition is "a dynamic ecological state of organisms living in aggregation characterized by sufficient mutual benefit to outweigh the disadvantages associated with crowding." In other words, a dynamic state of institutions working together for sufficient mutual benefit to outweigh the disadvantages or, phrased differently, the pain of not cooperating is worse than the pain of cooperating.

I will first give you the reasons to begin and participate in cooperative preservation microfilming projects; second, discuss the issues that have to be addressed in planning and implementing cooperative projects; third, offer some

---

Carolyn Harris is head of the Preservation Department at Columbia University Libraries.
[1]Robert Hayes, *The Magnitude, Costs and Benefits of the Preservation of Brittle Books* (Washington, D.C.: Council on Library Resources, 1987), p. 2.

models that cooperation has taken in the past; and fourth, talk about the pain of participating in such a project, ending with a few axioms.

In this context, I define a cooperative project as one that involves more than one person or institution working to preserve a body of materials by preservation microfilming following an articulated rationale.

ADVANTAGES

The point of cooperation is to work for mutual benefit. But what does that mean in pragmatic, practical terms? Most importantly, cooperation contributes to the preservation of embrittled materials; no one institution can do it all, so we work together for altruistic purposes. We want to provide continued access to materials that otherwise may be lost to all library users.

In a cooperative project, problems are solved collectively, using the pool of knowledge and experience. These solutions should lead to standards, guidelines, and manuals that have credibility in the larger population. Expertise is shared by members of a cooperative project, and there is access to training and educational opportunities.

Funding is often more forthcoming through cooperative action. A larger, more secure funding base may be available to a group than to an individual project. For example, the New York State Coordinated Grant Program specifically funds coordinated projects. Funding can also be used more efficiently; there is no need for every institution to reinvent the wheel. Raising outside funds can give a program internal credibility and provide the incentive to start up a program. If an external funding source sees a project as important, it must be.

A project requires institutional support, including space, staff, cataloging, materials selectors, equipment, supplies, and capital costs. This can lead to preservation becoming a priority within an organization. Peer pressure from other cooperating institutions can lead to internal support. Participating successfully in cooperative projects can improve your program's credibility among peer institutions and funding agencies by providing you with a strong track record of performance.

As a participant you may have access to centralized grant writing, budgeting, and money management. Participating also provides an opportunity to publicize your program on- and off-site, and to improve your public relations, especially within a larger context, e.g., a university community.

By-products of these projects are also important. They include retrospective conversion of the records for materials; an opportunity to acquire materials on film from other libraries, thus increasing access; and the opportunity to develop local and national priorities for preservation microfilming projects.

ISSUES TO BE CONSIDERED

A decision has been made to begin a cooperative project. What issues must be considered in designing and implementing a project? The primary ones concern planning and governance, participant responsibility and accountability, and the area of technical standards.

PLANNING AND GOVERNANCE

(1) The managing body must be identified. What organization or institution will govern the project? Will existing bodies take on this responsibility or will a new organization be set up? Is there strong central staff, institutional, or volunteer support?

(2) What is the goal of the project? How is it best articulated? Are you going to preserve all the maps of New York state, all German materials in research libraries, all brittle material in classics, all gazetteers, or all phone books? If it is a subject-based project, what will the subjects be? Are you going to address other categories: genre, format, language, imprint date or place, or a combination? In other words, what is the rationale of the project? Is it based on Association of Research Libraries conspectus values, on a specific subject, a specific format, locale, or imprint dates? Is it based on the interests of the funding sources when following their application guidelines?

(3) Should the project be centralized or decentralized? Is this a group of institutions doing their own projects under consistent guidelines, with funding going to each institution (e.g., the Art Materials Grant Project undertaken by the New York Public Library, New York University Library, and Columbia University Library), or are materials centrally chosen and decentrally filmed, or decentrally chosen and centrally filmed?

(4) Who will the participants be and how should they be identified? Should there be a "Request for Proposals" with a local option to participate? Should certain institutions be invited to participate, or "made to"? Should there be "chosen ones"? Look at the strengths of collections, staffing, and preservation programs. Should only the largest institutions do all the work?

(5) How will the project be funded? What funding sources are available and how can they be identified? Should the institutions who will benefit pay for it, or subscribers who want copies of the product, the National Endowment or another government funding source, private foundations? A combination? Who will actually write the grant if that avenue is selected?

(6) How will funding reach participants? Through the central office? On a recovery basis? Will funding be spent centrally for filming rather than distributed?

PARTICIPANT RESPONSIBILITY AND ACCOUNTABILITY

(1) What will institutions have to do to participate? How will you make sure they do it? What will their responsibility be? Can they meet the obligations?

(2) What is the estimated production rate? What are the local costs? How will the accounting be accomplished (e.g., quarterly reports)? How much will be paid per title, per volume, per exposure, per fiche?

(3) How will the product be distributed? How will access needs be met? The needs include both access to bibliographic information and access to the microfilms themselves.

TECHNICAL STANDARDS

(1) What technical standards will be used? Myron Chace's paper covers technical issues very well (see p. 35), as does the *RLG Preservation Manual* (2d ed., 1986). Both should be consulted in deciding what standards to set for a cooperative project.

(2) Will the project produce 35mm film, paper, or microfiche? Will all the production be identical? If so, what will the headers say? What fiche format will be used? What targets will be put on each film? How will each title be identified? How close will the production adhere to standards?

(3) Questions need to be answered relating to:
   (a) Preparation: Will pencil marks be erased or not? Will incomplete volumes be completed? Will volumes be cut (local option)? What sources will be searched?
   (b) Bibliographic control: Will records be entered on a network? Will titles be queued? Will full or recon cataloging be used?
   (c) Storage: Where will reels be stored and under what conditions?
   (d) Filming: How many duplicates will be made? How many printing masters? Will rigid specifications be followed? Will work be contracted out or done in-house? How many methylene blue tests will be run? How many density readings will be taken? Will the Quality Index test be administered? Will reels be inspected page by page? What type of film will be used? What reduction ratios will be used?

MODELS OF COOPERATIVE PROGRAMS

I have tried to raise questions, not be prescriptive. I cannot say what the answers are for your specific project. Cooperative projects have been around almost as long as there has been microfilming. I recommend Nancy Gwinn's article, "The Rise and Fall and Rise of Cooperative Projects" for a historical perspective.[1] I want to touch briefly on how these projects have been managed, or how the questions I have raised were answered in specific instances. All of these models, which vary widely, have been used successfully.

U.S. NEWSPAPER PROJECT

One of the earliest cooperative projects, which is ongoing, is the U.S. Newspaper Project. It was begun in the early 1970s by historians: the Committee on Bibliographical and Research Needs of the Organization of American Historians. The Committee began by starting a project to update the American Newspapers bibliography by Winifred Gregory (the National Endowment for the Humanities (NEH) funded that project). It soon became apparent that it was more than a bibliography project, and that library expertise was needed. As a result, the Library of Congress (LC) was asked to assist. The bibliographic part of the project became very complex, but the interesting aspect of this is that it did not start as a preservation project.[2] The Organization of American Historians realized that it did little good to have bibliographic records without having the materials extant, and preservation microfilming became a goal of the project.

With this project, there was an existing organization that identified the need and the resources, that developed an articulated goal to preserve all U.S. newspapers, that identified a funding source involved from the beginning, and that enlisted the expertise and support of the LC.

This model is centrally administered but decentralized in implementation. Clear guidelines are set by NEH and LC for participation by each state in the union. All states were invited to participate, but an institution within the state is required to make the application. All work is organized and accomplished within the state. Funding is awarded on an application basis, based on the guidelines, and the technical standards are those for traditional 35mm microfilming.

AMERICAN THEOLOGICAL LIBRARY ASSOCIATION

A second model is that of the American Theological Library Association (ATLA) preservation microfilming project.[3] ATLA itself took on the project management with paid staff. The project is centrally administered and centrally implemented. It is, however, funded decentrally and materials are selected decentrally.

---

[1]Nancy E. Gwinn, "The Rise and Fall and Rise of Cooperative Projects," *Library Resources & Technical Services* 29 (Jan.-Mar. 1985): 80–86.

[2]Harold Cannon, "The National Endowment for the Humanities and the U.S. Newspaper Program," *Cataloging and Classification Quarterly* 6 (Summer 1986): 7–13; Jeffrey Field, "The United States Newspaper Program", *CAN* no. 30 (July 1987): 5.

[3]Robert Markham, "Religion Converted to Microformat," *Microform Review* 16 (Summer 1987): 217–23.

ATLA began its preservation microfilming operation as early as 1955 with a serial project, and it has recently moved into monographic filming and increased its activity significantly.

The funding has come primarily from subscribers much like a commercial project with additions from NEH and others. ATLA has set criteria for eligibility of titles for filming, and subscribers may suggest titles that fit the criteria. A small group of large institutional subscribers suggests most titles. Staff also selects from the Union Theological Seminary and other subject bibliographies. Materials are requested from participating libraries, and the filming is accomplished centrally through contracts with the University of Chicago Library. The microfiche produced are distributed to subscribers for a low cost, or sold to non-subscribers at a slightly higher price.

ATLA clearly articulates its goal to preserve brittle religion materials; its planning is based on a survey clearly stating the need for preservation activity. The association is a strong group of libraries and librarians that have consistently cooperated with each other.

The formats chosen were 35mm roll microfilm for storage and microfiche for distribution. When the monographic project was started, the materials were filmed on 35mm roll film, then reformatted onto ultrafiche. This proved unsatisfactory for various reasons, production quality of the reformatted fiche being the major one, and, currently, fiche is being produced on step-and-repeat cameras.

AMERICAN PHILOLOGICAL ASSOCIATION

A project similar to ATLA's is that of the American Philological Association (APA).[1] An APA editorial board of faculty at campuses across the country was appointed to identify materials in classics that should be preserved within the brittle paper production time span. Funding was received from NEH and the Mellon Foundation. The filming was contracted to the Columbia University Libraries Preservation Department, and the books to be filmed were taken from the Columbia collection. Distribution at a low cost is being done by Scholars Press, which is a publishing arm of the American Council of Learned Societies based at Emory University.

The product is microfiche made by jacket-loading technology. Standards are the RLG technical standards. Payment to Columbia is made on a title- and fiche-produced basis.

---

[1] Roger Bagnall and Carolyn Harris, "Involving Scholars in Preservation Decisions: The Case of the Classicists," *Journal of Academic Librarianship* 14, (July 1987): 140–46.

CENTER FOR RESEARCH LIBRARIES FOREIGN MICROFILMING

A third model, with a somewhat different objective, is that of the Center for Research Libraries' (CRL) CAMP (Africana),[1] LAMP (Latin America),[2] and SEAM (Southeast Asia) projects. These projects were begun in the 1960s and 1970s both to increase access to materials and to preserve them.

The funding comes from subscription, with a minimal cost for copies of the materials. Each subscribing institution has a representative to a council that makes the selection decisions. CRL manages the projects and either has the materials filmed on-site (where the materials are) and purchases the film, or arranges for it to be filmed by the University of Chicago Libraries. Materials are usually housed in the country relating to each project, and North American access is an issue.

RESEARCH LIBRARIES GROUP
COOPERATIVE PRESERVATION MICROFILMING PROJECT

A fourth model is that of the Research Libraries Group (RLG) Cooperative Preservation Microfilming Project.[3] It is becoming the model for future projects of other organizations.

The Preservation Committee of RLG met in New Orleans in 1981. Out of that meeting grew the Cooperative Preservation Microfilming Project (CPMP). The type of organization involved and its governance dictated some aspects of the project.

The materials selected for the project were American imprints published from 1876 through 1900, later expanded to the period 1870 through 1920. The committee members felt that as a national organization, they should take responsibility for American materials. The first participants were institutions that had microfilming programs and would need little start up time. Based on strength of the various collections shown in the RLG conspectus, the subjects were divided up among ten participants. Each proposed their part: Brown filmed American poetry from the Harris collection; Columbia filmed the rest of American literature and language; Cornell selected American regional farm journals; New York Historical Library filmed travel, trial literature, and railroad history; the New York Public Library chose philosophy, religion, cultural anthropology, law, and medicine; Stanford worked on the history of the physical sciences; Berkeley and Yale filmed American history; the University of Michigan selected social sciences and technology; and the University of Minnesota filmed their Hess collection of dime novels.

---

[1]Ray Boylan and Cecilia Shores, "Collecting Retrospective Materials from Developing Nations: A Cooperative Approach through Microforms," *Library Acquisitions: Practice and Theory* 6 (1982): 211–19.
[2]Carl W. Deal, "The Latin American Microform Project: The First Decade," *Microform Review* 15 (Winter 1986): 22–28.
[3]*RLG Preservation Manual*, 2d ed. (Stanford, Calif.: Research Libraries Group, 1986).

It was decided to evaluate every U.S. imprint published within the period 1870 to 1920 housed in the collections in those subject areas. A curator (selector or bibliographer) reviewed the materials and, using his or her judgment, decided whether the volume was worthy of preservation. If no film already existed, the volume was filmed. If the volume were incomplete, libraries attempted to borrow the pages or volumes from another institution (members agreed to help each other out in this instance rather than going through interlibrary loan).

The RLG Board of Governors established an Advisory Committee that approved the direction of the project and the specific proposals. The project managers met extensively to determine the best ways to proceed. Out of this grew the RLG technical specifications and the guidelines for preparation, targets, searching, and bibliographic control that now make up the *RLG Preservation Manual* (2d ed., 1986) and have become *de facto* national specifications. Reimbursement was on a per-volume basis, based on estimated costs. Grant funds paid for the cost of the filming and half of preparation and cataloging costs, although, of course, the institution could allocate the funding as it wished, and it is now considered a lump sum payment. Each institution estimated their costs, which required a means of measuring the same operations, and resulted in the cost study as reported by Patti McClung.[1]

Also, out of this project grew the Preservation Scope Notes in the Conspectus, queuing, the ability to enter annotated records into RLIN at the point the decision is made to film, other enhancements to RLIN, and other projects.

The RLG project consists of the following components: strong subject collections defined within date parameters and proposed on a local initiative basis with a request for proposal going out to all members; a centrally written and administered grant; and work that is done to rigid production standards for 35mm polyester film (fiche could be acceptable) by local institutions who may opt to do the work in-house or through an outside contractor. A consultant visited each filming facility to determine if it would meet the standards. Filming duplication is avoided by searching and queuing on RLIN.

Three microfilm copies are made: the master camera negative is stored off-site at National Underground Storage (Boyars, Pennsylvania); a printing master is stored at the originating library; and a positive is held at the generating library as a service copy. All films are cataloged on RLIN.

Because this was the first cooperative project involving most of these institutions, upgrading of laboratory equipment and operations was often required. Most institutions did not have ultrasonic splicers or provision for methylene blue tests on a regular basis; some had to convert to polyester film. Preparation units had to upgrade or change their target-making apparatus and acquire an RLIN terminal and other searching tools.

At the time, project directors worked at ironing out their differences. Their first commitment was to a quality product produced in the most efficient manner that would last. The work has been very effective, but at the same time, changes

---

[1]Patricia A. McClung. "Costs Associated with Preservation Microfilming: Results of the Research Libraries Group Study," *Library Resources & Technical Services* 30 (Oct.–Dec. 1986): 363–74.

made over time are not always widely known. Always use the latest edition of the *RLG Preservation Manual.*

COMMITTEE ON INSTITUTIONAL COOPERATION

The first group to adopt the RLG model is the Committee on Institutional Cooperation (CIC), an organization of 11 major research libraries in the Midwest. The CIC Libraries have written a proposal for the funding of a major project. They applied for and received a planning grant to bring the participants together twice for two-day training and planning sessions. In some ways, they have varied from the RLG model: they have used a member institution to undertake project management; they have defined "brittle" and so will use a consistent measurement; they have established a technical advisory group; and they have made arrangements in case an institution could not meet its estimated goal.

NATIONAL LIBRARY OF MEDICINE

One of the most effective ways of completing a project is to have one institution film its own collection on the behalf of others. The National Library of Medicine (NLM) surveyed its collections and found that 8 to 12 per cent of the collection were brittle. This translated to 100,000 volumes, or 35 million pages. Congress appropriated $3.5 million to fund the project, and filming is underway. This filming will solve a large part of the brittle medical serials problem for the whole country. Along the way, it has been found that not all medical materials that need to be preserved are owned by NLM, and the library is working with the decentralized medical resource library system to cooperate further.

COMMISSION ON PRESERVATION AND ACCESS

A final model is what may be the most ambitious cooperative project yet, if funding becomes available. Patricia Battin, president of the Commission on Preservation and Access, is currently discussing a project to preserve the 3 million embrittled volumes identified by Hayes.[1] This plan would involve at least 20 research libraries producing 7,500 volumes a year each for 20 years. 150,000 volumes a year adds up to 3 million over the 20 years. Issues of governance, funding, and participation need to be addressed. Please stay tuned, and see what decisions are made.

ISSUES OF PARTICIPATION

What does it mean to be a participant in a program, based on one of these models, or a combination of models?

The most difficult problem in participating in a cooperative project is the tension between local priorities and national (or organizational) priorities. For example, the local priority may be the collection of East Asian materials, but

---

[1]Hayes, *The Magnitude, Costs and Benefits,* p. 2.

that subject is allocated to another institution. So the local priority may have to be something else. Identification of materials for preservation may not be your bibliographer's favorite task, public services may think that the cataloging department should give the processing of new materials a higher priority than microfilms (they inevitably do), upgrading a laboratory or contributing funds to support the project may not allow the purchase of personal computer work stations—and your user population may decide that you are destroying the collections and show great resistance to microfilm.

Other major issues of participation include:

(1) Developing the kind of institutional support needed. These are complex projects requiring coordination of many parts of the organization.

(2) Hiring and training qualified staff for a short-term project.

(3) Planning internal procedures, e.g., work flow, estimating costs and implementing and documenting the project with selectors, catalogers, and other supporting staff.

(4) Keeping up productivity in order to be promptly reimbursed.

(5) Acquiring and renovating space, purchasing and managing equipment, drafting contracts, making sure you have the ability to meet standards and are meeting them on a daily basis.

(6) Dealing with the usual problems required in the day-to-day management of bibliographic issues. It often seems that every volume presents some kind of problem: it is incomplete; it cannot be filmed bound and cannot be cut; or it is not the edition reflected in the records.

(7) Designing forms for statistics, keeping and reporting those statistics.

(8) Handling further complexities caused by research projects included in the grant proposal: in order to get funding a cost study or other analysis may be required. This sounds good but can cause significantly more work.

(9) Doing a full-time job in addition to managing a grant project.

(10) Ensuring smooth public relations within your organization, on your campus, or with your clientele.

CONCLUSION: AXIOMS FOR COOPERATIVE PROJECTS

Now you know why you should participate in a cooperative project, what some models are, what issues must be addressed, and what major difficulties will be encountered. To close, here are ten axioms of cooperative projects, all of which must be in place to be successful.

(1) an articulated common vision and goal;

(2) an energetic, competent, dedicated project manager;

(3) extensive planning;

(4) clear written specifications, standards, and guidelines;

(5) competent workers in a network of participants, who have the knowledge through adequate training and education to complete the project;

(6) administrative backing;

(7) articulated fiscal responsibility and accountability;

(8) adequate funding, especially from the local institution for the cost-sharing aspects of the project;

(9) an acronym, good publicity and public relations; and

(10) a commitment to a quality product.

One Step Beyond: The Future of Preservation Microfilming

Gay Walker

Almost everything to be said about this topic can be said in 15 or 20 words. They include: "project," "capacity," "efficiency," "database," "significant," "institutional," "cooperative," "digitization," "participation," and "management challenge." The combinations in which these significant words can be used are endless. With a slightly cloudy crystal ball and a great deal of speculation, I will explore some possibilities that may even be likelihoods, using a minimum of words many times over.

The preservation field has always grappled with two opposing forces: preservation and access, the yin and yang involved in all our efforts, particularly when considering the original item. To *preserve* the original is also to protect it, and when a volume merits physical protection as the primary preservation step, it inevitably results in a limitation of *access,* either immediately through transfer to a special collection or eventually as other copies deteriorate. The major movement within the field today, coming from both within and without, is the drive to microfilm deteriorated titles, to capture their contents on some more permanent medium while following recommended production and storage practices to the letter. The impact of this reformatting step on the original ranges from slight damage, at the least, to a more serious condition, a last-time viewing before disintegration. Based on a non-scientific survey of the field, the majority of filmed volumes are subsequently withdrawn from collections. While the majority of these same filmed volumes have little or no artifactual value and cannot be maintained in their deteriorated state, many should be and are. Some libraries withdraw all items filmed in preservation projects, some retain 5 to 10 per cent, some 40 to 60 per cent, and a few retain all, especially those filming in special collections or who loan to commercial reprinters. There are library volumes that contain a significant amount of information that can *only* be obtained from the original format. Both selection and preservation officers must be vigilant to identify and keep these special works.

Filming, on the other hand, captures the written intellectual content of deteriorated materials and allows greatly expanded access to them. This is true as long as the generating institution is absolutely conscientious in producing a *perfect* copy—not a copy where one page of advertising or one illustration caption or the colophon was skipped—and in providing appropriate storage and wide

Gay Walker is head, Preservation Department, Yale University Library.

distribution of that copy, upon demand, at a reasonable cost, and in perpetuity. When a brittle item is filmed, continued access to the original is limited and often totally denied; but access to the information is greatly expanded, and it is highly likely the original would be lost otherwise. In a case like this, the two Janus heads of preservation of and access to the information are melded together, dovetailing nicely with the national goal of preserving our written heritage.

A serious responsibility is assumed by all libraries that undertake the preservation microfilming of brittle materials. It can no longer be viewed as part of the local program to fulfill Professor Johnson's request. As long as the negative copy is listed in the National Register of Microform Masters/National Union Catalog (NRMM/NUC) or in a national database, it and your library are part of the national preservation program to preserve scholarly resources. That filmed copy must be a perfect one—other copies of the book will be discarded upon the strength of the listing. It is also likely to be the *only* time that volume will be being filmed and preserved. It must be done right the first time. A major concern about filming is that many filmed titles have missing pages, even though the film was inspected. One of the serious needs in this field is an automatic page proofer that can be programmed for illustrations and front and back matter.

Another important aspect of preservation microfilming programs involves the library's commitment to being a purveyor of goods. Upon receipt of an order, library staff will retrieve the film, copy it, package the copy, bill for it, and ship it—all for a nominal fee. A greatly increased demand seems likely as the number of titles filmed increases, and as both libraries and scholars undertake more searching and acquisition efforts. Some view this distribution step, the final endorsement and purpose of all these preservation efforts, to be an opportunity; others view it as a burden. Whichever, it takes staff and time and management.

There has been some discussion about start-up time, about space demands, about staffing difficulties, about training concerns and equipment problems, and methylene blue testing requirements and costs. Most of that information comes from sadder but wiser practitioners, but new participants can take advantage of their experience. This is also a national, or rather international, crisis of vast proportions. Each library taking up the torch is helping by chipping away at the problem. We might even be able to preserve almost everything, given the long shelf life of paper *after* it becomes brittle.

However, it is abundantly clear that all of the "gearing up" libraries must do, so that they can attack the problem with real vigor and undertake several times the amount of filming now underway, will not be easy. Space and staffing alone are a considerable hurdle for any library. If it takes one person to search, prepare, and catalog 700 to 800 volumes a year, where can you fit in ten more people needed for the job? Who trains them? Where do you get them?

Many libraries will be unable to provide space and time, or to absorb the 25-to-50 per cent of local cost-sharing expected in many grants. An all-important basic preservation program needs to be in place to support special filming projects if there is to be any buffer of staffing, or any work carried out in response to immediate local needs. Will the filming capacity be there when it is needed? Does every library need to gear up? All those who can do so with relative ease and competency should obviously do so. That expansion alone will not do the job, however. More money *could* become available than the actual (not the planned) programs can spend—given all the requirements and ground rules for this game, particularly in the area of staffing, space, start-up time, filming capacity, and costs.

What about digitization? What about optical disks, and digital analog disks, and read-and-write compact disks? The urge to undertake digitization projects that provide both preservation and access, but mostly access, exists now, particularly in the areas of special collections and collection development. But no one is saying those digitized volumes could then be withdrawn unless filming has also taken place, and this is a sticking place. A very powerful use of the digitizing technology can be made in preservation, in which the digitized text in a national database becomes a freely and widely distributed scholarly resource, and the microfilm becomes the archival format for consultation in the few essential cases where the additional information is required. So libraries would continue to film into the foreseeable future, capturing the essence of the book in a photographic image that is as true as possible to the original. As the digital database idea burgeons into projects, microfilms will be scanned, digitized, indexed, and made available to scholars everywhere through the ubiquitous database. Perhaps there will be no royalty charges, and it would truly be a scholarly library accessible to all, on a reader's personal terminal screen, through downloaded copies printed out locally, or through interlibrary loan networks.

New upon the scene is the composing/reduction camera, a highly versatile but very costly machine available on a custom order basis. It is capable of reformatting information into many formats, such as paper copy into microfilm or microfiche, microfilm into fiche, or any of these back into hard copy or into a digitized stream of information. It can both photograph and scan, and it *should* cost less to scan and digitize microfilm than it did to produce the film in the first place. The indexing required is a different matter and may prove much more expensive to provide. Although the high cost and great capacity of this machine constitute a major management challenge in keeping the workflow constant for efficient operation, it is encouraging that formats *can* be reformatted.

Even if digitization and the optical/compact disk technologies finally come through with a solid promise of materials longevity and resolution as crisp as that of the photographic, most of the procedural steps of staffing, training, and cost problems will remain. People will still be needed to prepare materials, run machines, index, catalog, and distribute, but particularly index. The new equipment and its maintenance costs would be significant, and an extraordinary vigilance would be required to protect and preserve that digitized text—between generations of hardware and software, through catastrophic electronic glitches, and from human tinkering.

These two technologies, the older microfilming and the current and future generations of electronic formats, could perhaps exist simultaneously but attain significantly different statuses. Neither would duplicate the purpose or goals of the other, and each would serve a definite scholarly need. Given the generally greater acceptance of computer terminals over microfilm readers and the confidence currently placed in the microfilm masters, this may not be so unimaginable.

Returning to the realities of today, experience with the practical problems of microfilm projects leads to examination of several cooperative models. This covers the spectrum from the individual library that carries out all the steps from A to Z (with some gathered expertise and *Preservation Microfilming*[1]), to a totally centralized filming operation (in which hundreds of libraries have no real local part) that films everything and sends out copies of any title needed at any time. The latter vision is highly attractive. Perhaps all libraries should donate resources to the Library of Congress to help it carry out such a program, but that is an unrealistic idea to solve the problem of filming many millions of volumes, perhaps in our lifetime. The Library of Congress has an excellent preservation microfilming program underway: they film approximately 11,000 volumes a year, and they are hoping to increase that number, but other personnel and other collections must be involved.

Portions of each of the cooperative programs are also appealing. The centralized grant-writing, reporting, and fund administration of the Research Libraries Group Cooperative Preservation Microfilming Project are attractive, as are the filming and storage services of the New England Document Conservation Center. The service, quality control, filming, research and development efforts, and cooperative support of the Mid-Atlantic Preservation Service (MAPS) look efficient. Moving towards the more centralized end of the scale, the volume identification, filming, cataloging, fund administration, project management, storage, and distribution provided by the American Theological Library Association (ATLA) program are most attractive.

In fact, the ATLA model suggests a number of distinct advantages. Efficiency can be pursued aggressively because of the clarity of focus and a status outside of the library, in effect, acting as a commercial vendor. The list of titles identified for filming can be selected in a number of ways: by a group of experts, from a bibliography, from various shelflists or printed catalogs, or in classification groups of subjects or call number ranges. Searching for available microforms can be done efficiently at the central location—with as much streamlining as possible. Any number of libraries can serve as host collections, and lists of needed titles could be circulated to participants, whose involvement would extend simply to verifying or obtaining the call number, pulling the title, and deciding to send and cut it for filming or not. Inputting the titles into a national database could be done centrally, as could the preparation, filming, inspecting, and record updating. Distribution could be handled immediately, and even storage could be undertaken at a commercial storage facility. The responsibility for continued distribution could be managed centrally or referred through individual libraries.

But how far can this model be taken—with a disparate group of libraries and no true national library that holds the authority, or necessarily wants to hold

---

[1]*Preservation Microfilming: A Guide for Librarians and Archivists,* ed. Nancy E. Gwinn. (Chicago: American Library Assn., 1987).

the authority, to command participation and to demand compliance with the ground rules of such a centralized system?

There is the Association of Research Libraries with its 118 or so members. It has a productive preservation committee and an interest in active preservation programs. As long as basic guidelines were followed, perhaps that group could administer funds from federal or foundation sources. Funds would be available to any member desirous and capable of being involved, patterned along the lines of the New York state preservation program in which legislated funds are distributed to libraries under a competitive grants program.

The Commission on Preservation and Access, the high-powered national group, is ready to provide leadership upon the clarification of the methodology. The goals are established, the logistics are still being refined. In order to film the three million plus deteriorated volumes identified as the target group for reformatting, monies, some or much of them federal, will need to be raised. With federal funding, constituency is always an important question. And constituency could be as broad as the *National Union Catalog* listings or a national database identifying title locations, anywhere in the country with a centrally-managed program. It appears that the broader the participant base, and therefore the perceived coverage of non-partisan and non-geographically limited book collections, the more likely that federal funding will be broadly supported.

This point argues for the development of regional facilities with centralized responsibilities and centralized funding. Such centralization would be a great boon to the established efforts in individual libraries. Local preservation programs could then address local needs and priorities, including special filming projects, and be freed of the necessity to expand quickly in this one area with its major growing pains, exacerbated by the soft money/fixed duration nature of grant funding.

A complete regional preservation microfilming facility could run fairly independently following pre-set guidelines. The facility would identify, search, and obtain titles, catalog and film them, and inspect and distribute the film, all managed internally. The fiscal and production aspects would naturally be of concern to the governing body, but each facility could be a self-contained unit. Subsidy would be necessary, but possibly at a lower rate than with current grant projects due to the vagaries of conditions, salaries, and problems among participating libraries.

An alternative to the above would be for all participating libraries not only to lend the materials to be filmed but also to pay for the positive copy and a bit more. Academic libraries, through a "preservation tax," could donate a minimal amount, say a partial percentage point of their acquisitions budget, to the Commission, who then would distribute those and federal funds to regional centers. The regional centers could be set up with grant funding but become self-supporting over time through centralized distribution of films. They might hold duplicate masters of all titles they film and obtain duplicate negatives from any other American libraries willing, and eager in many cases, to provide them. How many libraries are really covering their costs with those film orders? How many would miss the hassle of retrieval, reproduction, and billing for those copies?

It seems a very small step for a sponsor like ATLA, or even MAPS, to take on a few added responsibilities, but the responsibilities are major ones which require the kind of organized control present in ATLA with its directing board and member subscribers. So a fairly formal, authoritarian controlling body and fund administration would be needed; these elements could be provided by the Commission, the Library of Congress, the Association of Research Libraries, or by another group, if the desire were there to undertake the publicity and selling of the plan and the considerable effort to raise the money.

Let's look into my crystal ball at the year 2000, only 11 years away, but still an unknown in terms of technology and what we can expect for preservation. Digitizing is big business. Many projects involving digitizing have been carried out by both institutions and commercial vendors with hundreds of thousands of volumes. Images have been scanned, digitized, and made available online to any computer hooked up to a modem. The fight for free access to all parts of the scholarly library is still going on, but the database containing the institutional project efforts and a few of the commercial lists purchased by networks is accessible to all.

Brittle texts, particularly in the largest and most specialized collections, continue to be captured at the four regional preservation microfilming centers. The target population of deteriorated volumes came to over 5 million, but other materials, such as manuscripts, are also being handled. All centers are running efficiently, given the normal management problems. Since all the significant search tools for filmed titles are now online, it has been relatively easy for the regional centers to work through the shelflists of a handful of libraries and several major bibliographies. Large recon projects have also been tapped as identification tools for preservation filming, by checking tapes of titles having specific imprint dates against the database of filmed titles.

Most libraries have turned their local attention towards conservation treatments for rare and important works, the refurbishing and maintenance of stack collections, and the retention of reading copies in hard copy—now obtained primarily as a reprint, a computer output hard copy from the digital database, or as a paper output from the scanned film. Any order for a filmed title immediately instigates the scanning and digitizing of that film. Second and third sweeps of extensive subject collections and unique manuscript groups are the norm in local filming projects, and preservation units are increasingly involved in digitizing/access projects.

Read-and-write compact disks in a much denser format are now widely used and can be integrated into any personal computer with a hard disk drive. Disks may contain large numbers of texts in subject areas grouped by imprint dates, causing a significant change in the way scholars use resources.

But microfilming continues, and all films previously generated are being scanned and digitized and indexed over time. The two formats complement each other, and though optical digital disks are now considerably more permanent physically, the acceptance of a digital master is yet to come. Preservation specialists are beginning to feel more comfortable with their responsibility to ensure continued access to our written past—but pigeons still come through the fourth-floor windows, and Professor Smith still wants the book that is at the bindery—or the digitizer.

That short, but useful, list of opening words provides the conclusion: the significant institutional cooperative participation in the national centralized digitization and microfilm database project demonstrated efficiency, capacity, and our successful management challenge.